SAFE A

"What is important to me is people - even
landscapes are important because of what people
have done to them and so on. I'm particularly
involved with people who have no voice:
The dead, the dispossesed or the innarticulate
in various ways."

= fanthorpe's comment on her own anthology

The (flaunting) ⎫
The (silence)   ⎬ 3 examples of how
DNA   ⎭ Ⓕ hates moden life

- 2nd voice
- Humour
- Ref 2 past
    - ⊕ historical past — British
    - ⊕ architecture
    - ⊕ ⊕ "physical object
    - ⊕ a memory
- Some sort of criticism
    - (⊃) subtle references.

"I feel the need to rectify, to correct
the balance if I feel things are
un fair."

= fanthorpe's comment

This poetry communicates a positive
sense of life being worth living.
An affirmation of the value of the
existance of a human society which
is endlessly worthwhile.

↳ fanthorpes comment

Safe as Houses

U. A. FANTHORPE

How effectivly fanthorpe conveys

PETERLOO POETS

First published in 1995
by Peterloo Poets
2 Kelly Gardens, Calstock, Cornwall PL18 9SA, U.K.

© 1995 by U.A Fanthorpe

A catalogue record for this book is available
from the British Library

ISBN 1-871471-59-1

Printed in Great Britain by
Latimer Trend & Company Ltd, Plymouth

ACKNOWLEDGEMENTS are due to the editors of the following journals: *The Charleston Magazine, The Independent, North, Out of the Night, Poetry Review, The Printer's Devil, Prospero Poets, QLGF, Rialto, Seam, The Spectator, The Tyndale Society Journal, Windfall, The Winston Churchill School Clarion.*

I am particularly grateful for an Arts Council Writer's Bursary in 1994, and for a Cholmondeley Award from the Society of Authors, in 1995.

I should also like to thank Diana, Eddie and Di for their kindness and friendship.

For Rosmarie Bailey

Notes at top:

- Title
- Themes
- Language
- Images
- tone
- Own opinion

- intro
- eg 1
- eg 2
- eg 3
- concl.

Contents

THEMES

*All writers are products of their times

diff. structures {

*62 Atlas – Tribute 2 practical, real love
*63 The Absent-Minded Lover's Apology – mocking traditional form poem,
64 Sister – experience / innocent
*65 Christmas Presents – hope of humanity.
66 Cat in the Manger – Realism / comic / Religion
67 Christmas Sounds – Real value of christmas = secular world against religious world.
68 The Invitation – individual suffering.
69 The Wicked Fairy at the Manger – accepting ur fate.

TYPICAL FANTHORPE POEM

• Humour – twisting words
• Hidden message

RHYTHM + RHYME
(*lang, form, structure)
• no rhyme scheme (or 1/2 rhyme)
• different sized stanzas → inconsistant – unconvential.

*LANGUAGE
• confusing = ambigious
• complicated lang.
• harsh/soft sounds   } AO3 – at back.

Beast   sister.   (?)
                                          ussenance
• Syllables – set structure at end (sonnet)

FORM	STRUCTURE
• blank verse *STANZA	• how is sumin/c structured:
• poetry	– stanzas?
• prose	* how many?
• monologue	* lengths? in comparrison?

LANG
• alliteration
• assonance – rep of vowels
• antithesis – in one line – 2 opposite ideas – split
• hyperbole – exaggeration
• Metaphor
• Simile
• personification
• oxymoron – opposite words – 'silent noise'
• rhetoric – thought provoking qu – dsnt require answer – persuasive device
• Plosive – harsh words – empathises points
• Imagery – paints pic
• symbolism – symbol rep idea/feeling
• Onomatopia
• Punctuation – how pace of speech is controlled through punctuation
• PACE – of voice – tone changes
• Humour

• 2nd voice – who dominates poem – voice o

*LOOK UP
Ephram & Mercy

ancestors
haunting
us

generations gone by

Being in ghosts almost not visibly
reality & there
non-reality ur ancestors will always
be with you.

Haunting

ng
mbered

The ancestors. The shadow people, — part of you but dead
— Who now and then lean softly from the dark — past — come out 4 a
And stroke on chin or thumb the new generation. lil while

They aren't sure?! they are judging
affection/cussing influences
Mothers fear them, and their gifts, their talents. ur fam. may
Guessing half what they fear. *Who knows what you'll find* nt b at all
— If you look. Wreckers. And swindlers. The mothers are scared royal.
feared by mothers! about the traits & the
coz of influence on ur Fanthorpe — mums talents that are
Daredevil grans and presumptuous children and kids passed on
Ransack the archives. No treasure — pause — letdown — cliff hanger
But outlandish Christian names: Ephraim, Mercy. — outdated name
strange/weird collection of old things shows how religious.
look/hoping 4 glory dated relics
become
And tanned gigantic offspring from far-off historical England
Hoping, in holiday mood, for the Old Country, golden-age
For village blacksmiths, village greens and thatch, — trad. twee & trad
Sadden to find in faded sepia — colour-black&white chocolate boxy
The unpretending minutes of bleak lives. colour alone- twee
desc they find, lives of camera they come
of past — Doll-Imp never (les) back for a
a photo sence of catching holiday they
cry? hist as it want to come
tos abt is there home to c
mrs & then. the old country
but they don't

Even the noble, under his courtier's tiptoe,
Admits some fearful Berserk or Spreadeagler
As line-founder, and waits, tight-lipped,
For the claw to poke out from the lordly cradle.

linked to baby sence of enevitability
- devil
- evil
- primitive animals
- skeletons in our closet

person at the
of ur family
implies anncient Norse tied people up
malovance warrier who with their arms
faught with a and legs and
wild frenzy whipped to death)

xestorss seen as ghosts wou haunt our lives
oncluding stanza => Even people with status have things
ey dont like in their past.

Research - luk at T.S. Elliot => The Wasteland.

eiredutory & expectations.
vesthejate personal past physically present in
tho we dnt recognise it.

reflecting on our need 2 investigate the personal
past & how it is physically present in ur, though
we dont recognise it, so i rote the poem

The Silence

(for Jane Grenville)

I suppose it was always there, the strangeness.
Once on a patterned floor there was a god
With ears like lobster claws.
And those vast savage roads, stabbing
Like swords into distance. You could see how they
Hated the landscape.
Still there, but other things are taking root;
And still at times, through stripes of sun and shadow,
The stiff dead legions striding back.
Some of it I liked. The big town arch, those
Tall confident letters, the docked words,
Imp. Tit. Caes. Div. Aug.,
And so forth. Nonsense now. And toppled, I daresay.
Nobody goes there. One thing I remember
Of all their words.
A slave told me the yarn: some man, on his way
From losing a kingdom to finding another, gave
A friendly queen his story,

And her people stopped talking, and listened. *Conticuere omnes,*
Something like that. Stuck in my mind, somehow:
They all fell silent.

Nobody goes there now. Once it was full
Of tax-men, and gods, and experts
In this and that,

And the endless stone walls, sneering down,
Keeping out or keeping in? We'll never know.
And their magic unbudgeable mortar.

10

Handwritten annotations:

oxymoran - 2 choice of words that are opposit
juxtipation
2 words - one loud one silent.

→ no voice, not surprising - quiet.
→ implies history has no voice (link later)
↳ Referring to the fall of the R-Empire

monologue - poem - thoughts of one person

things left behind

← enjambement

simily ← violence

mosaeque — Roman style/med style
Repetition. existance
vicious — The roads
assonance - alteration with the vowls
segregation.
How they changed them into what they
armies. stress sig. on Romans - they made roads. wan
the roads purpose
monarch
other things built aswel
enlevelopment
the passing time.
Things have changed
cant escape them. death groups of soldiers. - recent past
The ruins
describing a tourist attraction
personifications
personified the ruins.
enjambement
Imperators (Titus) caesur div (Augustus) - Diller of R-empire.
litevally or the R. empire
olden Days - Roman story Aeneas
enjambemer
linked 2 a story by virgil (aeneid)
translation
ddnt have ne tink 2 say
(sbecame quite - can symb da fall of the R.empire.
literally the fall of the R-Empire
tone = conversationa
Priests
humourus.
combination
enjambement on same lev of hierarch
teesing horribleness
Hadrians Wall
nt everything refer 2 title.
cement - made it well
The things they did for us!
its still remains
To keep the English in Eng
scots out of Eng
her poetry deeds and art were 2 eng in a time
old certenties collapse
the contex new
stones - new

modern ppl r no good
wonder and intrigue —> ? <— *hadn arr well pa termed flee*
Romans

fanthorpe implies

we are not as good as the Romans

Strange beyond telling. They did so much,
Then turned their backs and left it. We, of course,
Can't keep it going, — *They came, did it, then left* — *modern*
cant handle it <-> *we cant evn keep it going*
go bk 2 old ways <-> *implies she prefers R. to the British*
No longer know their ways with central heating,
Water supply, and sewage,
And sickly babies. *medicine (new) — modern days — we rely ALOT on medicine*
in a packet — touch of a button
R. came along & recorded things b4 pre-history

They came too near the dark, for all their know-how. *Ready 4 use — lazy?*
Those curses they scratched widdershins on lead — *they knew abt bt & land some themselves*
Asking for trouble. / \ *anti clockwise direction*
or curses *in a certain fashion*
soc, even if in 4

We withdrew into the old places, that are easier *(sum) great & can ble n rule them.*
To believe in. Once we waited
For someone to come back, *rel. level — old rel & no rel. (ACtl) — waiting til a mertier & cvm ble*

But now it's clear they won't. Here we stand,
Between *Caes. Div. Aug.* and the next lot, expert only
At unspeakable things, *place us in history — but saying we cant ever gonna match up to them.*

Stranded between history and history, vague in-between people.
What we know will not be handed on. *— thing developed out*
Conticuere omnes. — *They all fell silent.*

— Sense of us only just having caught up with the Romans. — only improved little things.
— we are just catching up to their knowledge.

Conticuere omnes. (Aeneid II). Aeneas tells the story of the fall of Troy and his escape to
Queen Dido and her court at Carthage. These words describe the response of his listeners.
They were found scratched on a tile by excavators at Silchester, in North Hampshire.

poet reflects on a visit to Roman ruins, she considers
how far the Romans left their mark here in contrast
how she feels we will be remembered. — as experts — things
sense of wonder and intrigue at what the Romans achieved
long ago, and the feeling that they were afar superior
ble, than we will ever be.
Romans arrived in AD 43 to AD 410

The Room Where Everyone Goes

(Mount Grace Priory)

God's humour: uncouth helmet of silence;
God's blessing: hard cold water;
God's nursery: frigid stone.

His curriculum: spinning wheel; loom;
The word; and God, fidgety partner,
Fills the cell, or vacates it, at a whim.

Here we come, the inheritors, girt about with guidebooks.
Fast, prayer, solitude, face us like whips.
We try to imagine foot's curt patrol
Down each midget cloister; garden breath
Of mint and chives; the dished up smell
Of dinner the lay-brother left in the dog-leg hatch;
Holy sting of Latin in cold teeth
On dark mornings. Here, the monk's chair and bed,
Where we can sit or lie. Here, his window;
We can look out of it. How alien it all seems,
But for one spot, in the north wall,
At the end of the covered way. — *Ooh, look!*
The loo/the toilet/the bog! We run to see,
Take turns at sitting, feel (of course) at home.

Such cold, clean men.

The King's curriculum: ten monks from the London house
Chained hand and foot to Newgate posts
And left to rot (*Despatched by the hand of God,*
Said a careful cleric). Daily, a woman bribed her way in
With a bucket of meat, and fed them like fledglings;
(*Which having done, she afterwards took from them*
Their natural filth). In the end the gaoler panicked,
In the end (of course) they died.

12

They were always on sentry-go, never on leave
Drill, practice, training never stopped.
One way or other, they knew, God's inspection was coming.

judgement day.

They are out of reach. We can walk where they did,
But the guts and the goodness are beyond us.

we would not be able to handel that lifestyle.

Cold and godliness alienate. *The lack of understanding of*
The scent of the commonplace brings them home. *religion!*

The toilet, brings them home.

Mount Grace Priory =
In North Yorkshir, a working priory in the cleveland hills.

The toilet was the one thing that helped mom
feel less alienated was the toilet, as no
matter who you are everyone uses the toilet

the toilet connects past to present
↳ monks 2 us,

Notes

1. 'The Room Where Everyone Goes': I've borrowed this from W H Auden's 'The
Geography of the House':

> ... this white-tiled cabin
> Arabs call *the House where*
> *Everybody goes.*

2. The London house, i.e., the London Charterhouse. Founded in 1371, suppressed in 1538.

3. *A woman*: Margaret Clement (nee Gigs), adopted daughter of Sir Thomas More. When she
was prevented, she climbed to the roof and tried to let food down in a basket.

Tyndale in Darkness

For Michael Foot

> *ambitious/obsessed*
>
> Almost every good translation of the Bible ... has been undertaken
> by a single highly gifted zealot. Tyndale was executed before he
> could complete his task, but he set the English style ... which lives
> on in the King James Version (1611). A sacred book must be all of a
> piece, as though written by the hand of God Himself; and this can
> hardly happen unless a man of strong character, wide knowledge,
> and natural eloquence, working only for the love of God — perhaps
> under threat of death — sets his seal on it.

Robert Graves: *The Crane Bag*

St Jerome also translated the Bible into his mother tongue: why may
not we also?

William Tyndale

He translated the Bible into english but was executed before he did finish his task.

Translated Bible from Hebrew to english
↓
+ challenges power.

uses colloquial lang
↓
make every1 understand

14

[handwritten annotations, top margin: "is issued/withr/persecuted = bcoz spread word of God", "parably Jesus", "Hebrew text", "nearest one linked to Jewdaism", "Old way – culture of time = unforgivable God", "forgiving God"]

TUESDAY

Defecerunt sicut fumus dies mei et ossa mea sicut gremium aruerunt.
(My days are consumed like smoke, and my bones are burned as an hearth)
(Ps 102: 3)

The Old isn't as easy as the New.
Greek's nothing, but I needed Germany
To teach me Hebrew. Then the endless trail
That drags from Genesis to Malachi!
Now the New's finished, printed, launched on the world,
Doing its work in England, in plain English,
All clinched and Bristol fashion. But I
Not there to see it. Flushed out
From Gloucestershire first by a rout of clownish priests

> Who, because they are unlearned, when they come together to the
> ale-house, which is their preaching-place, they affirm that my
> sayings are heresy.

[handwritten: quote Tyndale (1886)]

Then in London, bluffed, swindled, bullied,
Hounded at last abroad.
        Well, God's work
Can be done here too, though I miss the rough sweetness
Of English. But on the run always, always I need more time,
Space, books and peace to do things properly.
And light, and warmth. These I miss here
In my palatial jail, the Emperor's guest.
Still, I can get things done. But how I grieve
The watery deathbed of my Pentateuch
In the deep roadsteads off Holland. Back to the start
Again. I did them all again. All five.
But it held me back. Here I am now
Still toiling through the waste of Chronicles,
When I could be at the Psalms, dealing with hope,
Injury, loss, despair, treachery, joy,
Not endless histories, churned out by some
Dull priest with a long memory. Only five books to go
But how long have I? I get used to Death

[handwritten annotations in right margin and throughout: "testament – collections of parables", "translating them into eng", "old & new testaments", "old testament", "printing launched on the world (colophon 53)", "in his own country", "he died B4 he old finish", "bringing in colloquialism", "got sent out of England...", "maybe translating in another language?", "I killed Jews WW2"]

[handwritten bottom: "Its a risk for him to carry on writing them out as there is the punishment of death."]

15

Leaning over my shoulder, with his noose and brand,
Breathing at each sentence end. I know he waits his day,
But not the day itself. I doubt I'll ever reach
So far as the happy man who's like a tree
Planted by water, that brings forth his fruit in its season,
And look, whatsoever he doeth, it shall prosper.
Well, Miles gets the Psalms. My heir. He'll bring forth his fruit,
The happy man. But I too was planted by water,
Born with the tune of Gloucestershire in my head,
Knowing our English as much the language of heaven
As Jerome's tawdry Latin, pagan patter,
That Jesus and His fishers never spoke.

They say it cannot be translated into our tongue it is so rude. It is
not so rude as they are false liars. For the Greek tongue agreeeth
more with the English than with the Latin. And the properties of
the Hebrew tongue agreeeth a thousand times more with the
English than with the Latin.

Not many days left me, not many days.
They keep my working books, my Hebrew Bible,
Grammar and dictionary. I'd get on faster
If I had them, and light to work in the dark.
Sicut fumus dies mei, my days are consumed —
Consumed? An empty word. *Eaten* is better.
Defecerunt. Bloodless Latin! But English lives!
Will Miles be up to it? — yes, eaten
Like smoke, and smoke will finish me
Here, in the marketplace at Vilvorde. *Et ossa mea* —
And my bones burned up like a hearth.
That too. But here, while I live, in the cold and the dark,
I long for a whole shirt, and a lamp at night.

I suffer greatly from cold in the head, and am afflicted by a
perpetual catarrh ... My overcoat is worn out; my shirts are also

16

worn out ... And I ask to be allowed to have a lamp in the evening;
it is indeed wearisome sitting alone in the dark.

WEDNESDAY

Vigilavi et factus sum sicut passer solitarius in tecto
(I watch, and am as a sparrow alone upon the house top)
(Ps 102: 7)

He is the sparrow, the Friday lord.
I hoped to be the watcher on the rooftop,
But He was first. I'm flake of His fire,
Leaf-tip on His world-tree.
                                        But I watch too,
As once I stood on Nibley Knoll and looked
Out over moody Severn across the Forest
To the strangeness of Wales, Malvern's blue bony hills,
And down on the dear preoccupied people
Inching along to Gloucester, the trows with their sopping decks
Running from Bristol with the weather behind them,
And none of them knowing God's meaning, what He said to them,
Save filtered through bookish lips that never learnt
To splice a rope or fill a bucket. So I watched,
And saw the souls on the road, the souls on the river,
Were the ones Jesus loved. I saw that. Now I see
The landscape of my life, and how that seeing
Has brought me to this place, and what comes after.
So He saw the history of us, His people,
From Olivet. And told His men to watch.
*Vigilate ergo (nescitis enim quando dominus domus veniat; sero, an
media nocte, an galli canto, an mane), ne cum venerit repente, inveniat
vos dormientes.* *
They couldn't keep their eyes open, poor souls.
Vigilate. As well tell them to stand on their heads.
Erant enim oculi eorum gravati. For their eyes were heavy.
I doubt I'd have done much better.
It must have been a hard day for them,
And they weren't used to late nights, the disciples,
But to early mornings, when the shoals come in.

17

Hard-headed men with blisters on their palms
From the nets. Why did He ask them to stay awake
When He knew they couldn't? Because He always does.
He picks the amateurs who follow Him
For love, not devout professionals
With a safe pair of hands. Look at Peter,
A man permanently in hot water, chosen,
Perhaps, for that very thing. God sets His mark
On us all. You start, and it's easy:
I heard the ploughboy whistling under Coombe Hill,
And I thought, *I could do that.* Give him God's word,
I mean, in his own workaday words. And I did,
But it got so difficult: exile, hardship, shipwreck,
Spies everywhere. Then prison, and the fire.
God's mark on me, as on Peter. I would have slept, too.

THURSDAY

King Henry opposes w̄g
Ꝙ is doing

Principes persecuti sunt me gratis.
(Princes have persecuted me without a cause)
(Ps 119: 161)

What can you do with power except misuse it?
Being so mighty makes these men afraid
That we, their subjects, might guess they're men too.
That I can understand. It's the followers
Who turn my stomach. The glib climbers
Greedy for money, land, influence, jobs for the boys.
They're drawn by the power and the glory,
And kings aren't fastidious. Consider Henry's men —
Cuthbert the cloth-eared Bishop of London;
Wolsey the Suffolk wolf; and foul-mouthed More,
The bitterest tongue in England. Consider also
Their noble master Henry, the subject-harrier,
Who drove me here. Well then, consider them.
They fear me. So they should. I plan
The invasion of England by the word of God.
And it will come. Just now, they burn my books.
An easy step from that to burning clerks,

18

Burning this clerk for doing what God wants,
Turning God's word to King's English.

                                        But not the King's;
The people's; England's English. That's where Christ is.
Not a king to do business with Popes and chancellors,
But a servant, a man beneath us, who washes our feet,
Who goes before to try out the hard things first,
Who opens gates so we can go easily through,
That is the king, one and only, who speaks our own words.
The powerlessness and the glory.

Princes have persecuted me. Perhaps they have a cause.

Jesus died on Friday – before (T)'s death (stained).

FRIDAY

Scribantur haec in generationem alteram et populus qui creabitur laudabit Dominum.
(This shall be written for those that come after: and the people which shall be born shall praise
the Lord)
(Ps 102: 18)

The powerlessness. This is the day He dies,
Jesus, the Friday sparrow, the watcher on the cross
Who forgives those who put Him there. He's dying now,
And His world is dying too. I made this world twice
After God; twice I translated Genesis. I know
The deep places in it. And God said,
Let there be light, and there was light.
The accurate voice of God. And after Him, me;
Tyndale of Nibley. The human small-scale words
For the unimagined thing. And as Jesus hangs dying,
That same immense familiar light, that shines
Over Nibley and Bristol, London and Flanders,
Over all the countries we know glancingly of,
Goes out, as the world, more faithful than its people,
Mourns for its maker. The world itself dies.

19

God says, Let there be no light.
And when the sixth hour was come, there was darkness over the
                  whole land until the ninth hour.
Starlings think it night, celandines shut their petals,
Trees in Westridge Wood stand frostily waiting.
No light. No light. God said, Let there be no light,
While Jesus is dying.
                  I want to die like that,
Brave and forgiving. I may not be able.
The grace is not in us. We have to ask.

We must also desire God day and night instantly to open our eyes.

So little time. We have to hustle God
Who, in His unhorizoned sphere of time,
Can hardly know how short our seasons are.
And I pray too for resurrection in the word.
This shall be written for those who come after.
And still, these tedious Chronicles waiting for me,
These kings and priests and rulers of this world,
These Jeroboams and Jehoiakims,
Between me and *beatus vir*, the happy man,
Whose leaf shall not wither. Unlike mine.
And look, whatsoever he doeth it shall prosper.
Et omnia quaecumque faciet prosperabuntur.
Prosperabuntur? God's teeth, what a word
For Christian tongues to wrestle with. Language for liars!
Our dear and patient English shall rip out
The rubbish Jerome stuffed in the Church's mouth.
I must get on. Day and night. Instantly.
The Psalms are waiting. So are the English.
Vile the place is, but still my Father's house.
Lampless or not, He lights it.

---

* Watch ye therefore, for ye know not when the master of the house cometh, at even, or at midnight, or at the cockcrowing, or in the morning: lest coming suddenly he find you sleeping.

Tyndale in Darkness: Notes

Who, because ... are heresy: Tyndale, quoted in Demaus, *William Tindale*, London, 1886.

The Emperor: Charles V.

My Pentateuch: Tyndale's first translation of this was lost when his boat sank.

The happy man: Psalm 1.i. Blessed is the man that walketh not in the counsel of the ungodly ... he shall be like a tree planted by the rivers of water.

Miles: Miles Coverdale, who worked with Tyndale and took over at his death. *The Book of Common Prayer* Psalms are Coverdale's.

Jerome: Translated the Old and New Testaments from Hebrew and Greek into Latin (the Vulgate).

They say ... with the Latin: From Tyndale's *The Obedience of a Christian Man*.

Vilvorde: Where, in 1536, Tyndale was strangled and burned.

I suffer ... in the dark: Letter from Tyndale, imprisoned in Vilvorde Castle.

Nibley Knoll: in South Gloucestershire, where the Tyndale Monument now stands.

Trows: Severn barges.

Vigilate ergo ... dormientes: Matthew 24.42.

Erant ... gravati: Matthew 26.43.

Cuthbert: Cuthbert Tunstall, Bishop of London.

More: Sir Thomas More was more vituperative in polemic even than Tyndale — which is saying something!

Twice ... Genesis: The first translation was lost in the Rhine shipwreck.

And when ... ninth hour: Mark15.33.

Westridge Wood: On the ridge above North Nibley.

We must also ... our eyes: From Tyndale's *A Prologue*.

The Doll's Children

annotations: — REP - mothers — wnt to stay young.
artificial image
innocence / experience

> I have been your doll wife, just as at home I was Daddy's doll child. And the children in turn have been my dolls.
> Ibsen, *A Doll's House*

annotations: mother is seen from children's perspective as immature and embarrassing

not alone

CRITICAL TONE

We are the children of the doll,
Our mother plays sweetly with our toys,
She is better at childhood than we are.
O mother! with your <u>little</u> feet and your <u>little</u> fingers,
Your <u>sweet</u> tooth, your <u>pretty</u> ignorance,
Your laughing and shrieking and hiding under the table,
Your tambourine and your <u>tarantella,</u>
Shouldn't you have grown up by now?
We <u>need</u> to explore the casual ways of childhood;
You are so professional, you take up all the room.

annotations: children unable to experience a 'proper' childhood / childish charactoristic / critical / drags out sentence / childish connect / (peasant dance) / bitter tone / 1/2 rhyme - conveys dissatisfaction at being child / Plea

(father in a Doll's House - Ibsen's play)

We are the children of the <u>Bank Manager</u>,
Whose job it is to be <u>master</u>,
Who is surrounded by people
Who are softer and smaller than he is.
This is the man who understands audits,
Debit and credit and profit and loss,
Who never listens or understands,
Whose <u>children</u> stay babies,
Who married a <u>skylark</u>,
Who <u>lives in the house that he built.</u>

annotations: authority / Ironic: understands monetary gain/loss but cannot c how he is losing his wife/family / sense that parents are not allowing children to grow up / narrators of stanza / bird of freedom / he has made family what they are.

left margin: pronounced rhythm of this stanza reflects child's nursery rhyme - the house that Jack built.

We are the children of this house.
We sit on <u>dinky</u> chairs, at <u>dinky</u> tables,
Speaking <u>gingerbread language.</u>
We are afraid, mother, father, we are afraid.
Some day we shall <u>turn gawky</u>,
<u>Voices will break, hair and blood</u>
<u>Spring from unchildish places.</u>
How will you go on loving us then, you who need us
To be younger than you?
When shall we see your faint suspicion
That we have betrayed you, becoming ourselves?

annotations: like dolls - never grow up / link to Hansel & Gretal / ref. to puberty: parents dont want them to grow up/awkward. / the children maturing / Puberty: Loss of innocence. / parents need children to stay young so they can stay young ⟹ stop time.

enjambement - conveys a sense of uncertainty and suspense related to puberty.

* The day the children grow up they will betray their
22 parents who have tried to protect and isolate them
⟹ parents dont wna let their children go ⟹ keep young 4ever

The mother in 'A Dolls House' – Ibsens play

We are the children of Norah,   *ref. to plot – turn her back*
Who walked out of the doll's house   *on family*
Into a city unfriendly to skylarks and squirrels, *mother + father*
Whose dance-halls were shady, *real – not a perfect world*
Whose cake-shops were shut; *like a dolls house*
We are the children of Norah who slammed the front door, *mother seen finally as*
Who walked out alone with her courage *courageous and*
As the youngest son walks alone into the forest. *single-minded.* *metaphor for life*
We were the children of the doll;
ular It seems there is hope for us, after all. *full rhyme conveys a sence of-certainty, finality, inevitability.*

etition
past tense shows children no longer belong to mother,

positive ending as children grow up.

oem inspired by Ibsen's pay – 'A Doll's House'.
oem takes form of a dramatic monalogue -
Uses 'we' not 'I' though.

MES/IDEAS
gives voice to children/inarticulate
rotection/restriction → how to bring up a child
arent/child relationships
rotection/restriction of houses (symbolically)
rowing up/maturing.
ouses are a dominant image which both restrict & offer
ection – the house in Hansel & Gretal was a) not real
weet + pretty on outside – but evil on the inside

ouses appears as images throughout:
the Dolls House
The House that Jack built
The 'gingerbread' House

The house was an illusion

MINIST READING
omen (Norah) regains independence
raditionally women stay at home & cook, clean, care
children, the dominant man goes to work → through
racters – UAF criticises this ideal & shows how when a
men is happy, free and fullfilled she becomes a
tter role model/mother.

Reading between

'It is perfectly true, as philosophers say, that life must be understood backwards. But they forget the other proposition, that it must be lived forwards.'
Kierkegaard, *Journals*.

Novelists were no help. They made you think.
Mr Joyce, so difficult; Mr Lawrence, so coarse;
And Mrs Woolf, so strange. But these
Were the kindly ones, whose gift was
To immobilise memory.

So much to face: bald war-memorials;
One-armed men at stations selling matches;
Failing chicken-farms; little mad mothers
Muttering at bus-stops.

But these were the code-breakers; these gave answers.
In locked rooms, in libraries, one man
Dies for the people. Not in random shambles,
But stylishly, slugged on the left temple
With a blunt instrument.

These civilised Death. Such singular corpses
Could be coaxed into downright discourse:
Rigor mortis; finger prints; contents of stomach.
Nothing to mourn here.

The police, thick-witted, true-blue,
Are on our side; and their unlikely allies,
Foreigner, with accent; unimportant old lady
With knitting; nervy nobleman
With heirloom brains.

No doubt they guessed what was coming. They knew
History's unreliable narrators, Europe's locked room,
Poor bloody little Belgians. Identical twins, unclassified poisons —
There was no irregularity they hadn't charted.

24

[handwritten annotations: change in tone = war; colloquial; because it was so bad, we kept believing it's true; Boer War]

And yet of course there was: the colossal one
On the edge of being true, Auschwitz, the Burma Road,
Hiroshima, all that followed. Perhaps they chose
Not to tell, being creators of small occasions,
Of problems with answers.

O rare little world, where a biking bobby *[nostalgia — policeman on bike]*
Is about to spot that open window; where Whitehall 1212 *[operators on the phone]*
Is the number to ring; where golfing colonels *[only mes.]*
Are ready to say *Eh what?* and nice girls
Like being rescued, *[— damsel in distress]*

O rare little world, *[— comes back down]*
Imagined to gentle the English through war, *[— WW1]*
And Depression, and war, and peace, and anything else, *[— what the harshness was]*
Cheap, unpretending, with your faith in solutions,
O Never-Never world, not to be read twice.

[handwritten notes:
1930's   WW2
— Peter Pan — unwilling to face reality.
James Joyce — Ulysses
DH Lawrence —
Virginia Woolf — the lighthouse

The Past glosses over the harshness of the war. She tries to expose this.]

25

Annotations (handwritten): the Blitz ↑ a warning | pun on siren | Reflects to air-raid siren | ← winged creatures controlled by human mind (Greek mythology) -Syren / -winged women who sang to sailors to their death on the rocks | air raid warning siren

Sirensong

(for David)

'What song the Syrens sang...'
Sir Thomas Browne, *Urne Buriall*

Annotations: - monologue - poet? | sets the scene: poem abt war memories | sound of bird song | onamatopeia | Community: normally they wldn't help : effects of wartime on community / sense of being in | colloquial: Potatoes | no point => all fortunes were same | dying has becom more acceptable - everyone is destined to death | enjambment blurs, increases sence of anticipation | capitals for emphasis childish | still can't say words | always felt safe there | cliché - title of book | post WW1 | WW2 | Personification

I know the <u>song they sang</u>. I heard it,
The husky (warbling) on the <u>war's first day</u>.
I learned the meaning, too. *Lie low, lie low.*
<u>Gipsy women</u> came to the door for help
With ration books they couldn't read. They gave us
<u>Spuds from giant baskets; told no fortunes</u>
(All fortunes were the same). Endlessly Mother
Explained about The (Will), and who
Would take us on, if anything ...
Ours had been a <u>safe house</u>. Safe as houses
Ever are. Built in a <u>post-war country</u>
(P) It stood up straight, untroubled by rumours of <u>war</u>.

Annotations: B4 - things were perfect! | house remembered vivid thru child's sense of touc | no more faith in God : there is no need | sence of belonging | The safe house wasnt safe (irony) | our plans are not controlled by | delicate - like bird | vivid imagery - only shells are left | this was their playgrnd | death/destruc became inevitable | don't talk abt death/defeat. | very philosophical | fireplace | destroyed walls | house no longer safe | desperate image | the bedroom the bathroom

My baby knees crawled through it, certain of polished párquet,
Turkey carpets, quarry-tiled kitchen floor.
My knees understood this was a forever house.
The <u>end of faith</u> in brick. The house fluttered,
As <u>trespassing aircraft droned life-long</u> overhead,
Leaving the town rubble and honeycomb.
We were <u>precocious experts</u> on shrapnel and blast.
Things broken weren't replaced. <u>What was the point?</u>
Friends were lost, too. <u>You didn't talk of it.</u>
We knew <u>how bombs sliced off a house's flank,</u>
Uncovering private parts; how bedroom grates
Still stuck to walls though wallpaper (flailed) outside;

Annotations: everything has been exposed | SAFE HOUSE: a place of refuge / rendevous | SAFE AS HOUSES: expression of British origin meaning thoroughly and completely safe.

26

How <u>baths</u> slewed rudely, rakishly into (view;)

sip — How people noted, and talked of what they saw; ½ rhyme —

pple talked — How ours might be the next; and what they'd say conveys a sense
their   Tone becomes v. melancholy / of things gone
ses   depressing missing /
    Peace made no difference. Still too young to matter, gone / going
ays   Someone <u>still fighting somewhere</u>, some children wrong!
ar   Are <u>invaded</u> for ever, <u>will never learn to be young.</u>— childhood lost
    to war — UAF?
unty? — Their minds remain invaded 4eva
   — corrupted / brainwashed / troubled?

We missed the jazz and swing of our extrovert parents,
The pyrotechnic raves of our <u>groovy</u> kids. youthful language.
Our <u>ground was never steady</u> underfoot.

ear wax?
We had <u>no wax</u> to cancel the sirens' song: — to block out sound of song.

Lie low, lie low.   did not 4get the sound — the soldiers put wax in their ears so they didn't hear the sirens.

They neva had the chance to be young and carefree like their parents and their children bcoz their minds were so full of war.

<u>emes / Images</u>

here is no escape from memories for children brought
in the war.

oem explores destruction of war and the effect it has
people left behind — always focus on soldiers

n wartime, children don't get to be carefree ⇒ houses are
longer safe. — people help each other — link to 'Collateral Damage'

he house is frequently personified in a grimly comic way —
un on private parts.

ME — WAR — the importance of a house during war.

nounces importance of a house: 'our house fluttered' ⇐ v. delicate
⇒ not stable
⇒ not safe.
(3),
se strong during peace - safe: (4), (5)

(handwritten top:) comparison to a soldier dying and autumn/fall

(margin left handwritten:) evoked from watching a parade

(handwritten above title:) Autumn / death of a coz of war. / soldier / haircolour — colour associated with Autumn / alliteration of 'G'

Dying Fall

(handwritten:) The leaves fall on the floor

(margin:) remembrance day / "July"

November's leaves flock ginger and stiff along the gutter,
Waiting for the wind to say. —

(handwritten:) death / personification / trenches

(margin:) personification

Boots (black), shoes (brown), knee-socks (white)
Their feet speak for them:

(handwritten:) list of 3 / check list ! = BRACKET

(handwritten:) The marching / uplifting sense of pride / millitary feel.

(margin:) youth

Brownies and cubs (eyes left to grin at Mum), — looking for the support
WRVS, swinging arms whose baskets we know,

(handwritten:) womens royal voluntary service (WW2) / rural countryside. / innocent + youth

Guides, Scouts, Sea Scouts, all different, all tweaked
Into step by the bully band,

(handwritten:) list of 3 / no individuality - just another number / featureless children / basket d

(margin:) soldiers = volunteer to fight & die.

And the band's irresistible, dammit. I choose not to conform,
I don't want to fight, but by jingo jingo jingo ...

(handwritten:) colloquial / anti-war speech / mild oath - like 'god damn it' / patriarchal viel / pompous/colloquial / dont conform in life = rebellious

(margin:) idea that music + emotion of a soldier = marching

Thin irregular pipe of peace, please. Not this rude
Heartbeat that fuses us all

(handwritten:) silence / alliteration / flaunting / silence = loss of G / in air no / - Reeling shook identity / not C

(margin:) old men soldiers

With the bowler-hatted grey shufflers and their hulking flag,
Grasped cack-handed in a gauntlet,

(handwritten:) The old men that are finding it hard to hold it and do the para / the union jack / awkward + clumsy / glove to hold the flag →

(margin:) memorial stones

And the washed dim names that no one remembers,
Who died in a muddle of bugle-calls

(handwritten:) sense of chaos and confussion / The last post! - mark of death / grass / idea of

(margin:) old men died

And the fitful drumbeat of glory,
Ending up, like the leaves, in mud,

(handwritten:) one soilder = one left / in the mud / autumn / Brings the poem back full circle.

(margin:) Sinister image

Skulls, tongueless bells, miming their message,
Waiting for the wind to say.

(handwritten:) The soilders dont have a vioce / sinister pics.

(handwritten bottom:) die in first with first 2 stanzas / voice less ing / poem comes full circle. / personification / tone = very sinister / we all know how bad war is but we still hold rememberence 2 them - a celebration / fanthorpe tries to give the toungless soilders a voi... / ↑ anti war msg.

28

(footnote handwritten:) *UAF anti-war, noone remembers the people. All the honour/goodness is rubbish - it is not honourable to die + being remembered is not honourable eith...

Town = flooded by water to create a dam! Mardale! | collateral damage | everything destroyed

* Neg. effects on children in war. — wa kind of govt cld allow this — tiny r safe real ppl die.

Collateral Damage
— destruction or injury beyond that intended or expected!

The minor diplomat who brings terms for a ceasefire — during a war
Enters through a side-door, in the small hours,
Wearing a belted raincoat. — trench coats

> tiny diplomat rep govt
> *SINISTER IMAGES
> late nite / early morning

The children have become bold. At the first siren
They cried, and ran for their mothers.
Now they are worldly-wise, — they are more used to the war

> bcoz of war — mouthy
> saying too much war = sinister made them (worldly-wise)

They clamour to watch dogfights above the house, — growing up with the war!
— They prefer under-the-kitchen-table to the shelter,
They play fighting games — trying to be grown up — not playing child games
Of reading the paper by bomblight, — shld be candle light, sinister
Pretending to be the enemy. These children — ENJAMBMENT humour tone!
Are no longer safe. — They have lost their innocence

> close combat between to planes
> childhood turned into entertainment — combat btwn fighter aircrafts.
> not like the houses which are not safe either
> thru making serious point empathises/warning. longing

They have learned rash and contrary for ever. Come soon,
O minor diplomat in the belted raincoat, come (E)
To capitulate. For the children have ack-ack nerves, — nerves like guns.
And a landmine has fallen next door. (anti aircraft guns onomatopeic — broken)

> next door bombed
> *stanza = reminder of destruction
> double space = change of tone.

Under the reservoir, under the wind-figured water, — under the motorway/lasthouse
Are the walls, the church, the houses,
The small human things, — list of 3

> if there was a drought the houses wld still be there
> really min — ghost-like.

That in drought rise up gaunt and dripping,
And it was once Mardale, both is and is not Mardale,
But is still there, — The houses are still there

> submerged village in Lake district.

Like the diplomat, and the crazy fearless children = corrupted! of war
Who progress through their proper stages, and the churchbells — experience of war made them fearless
With their nightly riddles, — a curfew! — ring at certain time — break curfew

> everything it all seen it all — of war.
> children still running rings of bombs

And the diplomat, and the children still running — children still running
Away from shelter, into the path of the bomb.

> sense of urgency
> shelter thought not safe
> running to death.
> no hope — use of commas and the world AND, gives it a fast past sense of inevitability.

29

> mar — feeling of speed.
> go — wa kind childhood is this — lasthouse.
> sies on festiver destruction
> under the table — in (banns way)

watching a cinema being destroyed

Last House – picture house = Cinema

in detail / almost as if in slow motion – languid, lazy, 'hum' 'waver' 'flops' 'stills'

Like the dead march, the beat of destruction is slow. —
The crane-man stirs; the giant ball moves over; destruction
A hum; a waver; a trickle of mortar; a pause; – as though exhausted
A slice of wall flops over out of the sun.

to go unsteady
This is the last performance. The Regal yaws doubtfully   cinema
As audiences do, wanting the star to fall, actor? cinema?
But not till the last reel, at sunset, to the right music,
scene   dance? – "in the limelight".

The crowd remembers whistling in limelit smoke, – old cinema : yo
Organist rising astride his yodelling nag, organ   old smoke / dim l
Usherettes with torches and no-nonsense style, } +traditional image
Chocolates, cigarettes, trayclad girl in a spotlight, } of cinema
↳ 2nd voice – usher

'crumpled 'folded 'bent

—Buckled backseat couples, gauging how far they can go,
Persistent men in macs at matinees, sordid implications
Lustrous magnified eyes oozing slow motion tears, } range of
Hi-ho-ing dwarfs, hi-yo-ing cowboys, Hitchcock. } cinematic emotions/express

from Casablanca   impassive/stiff
Here once they studied poker-faced dialogue
(Here's lookin' at ya, kid); here they learnt   Dustin Hoffman
How to sing in the rain; to hamlet; to tootsie; to catch 22; — Joseph Heller
How to make passionate love to Elizabeth Taylor.   ← also show
famous plays/films used as verbs – comic effect   impact of cinem
on culture and fashion

Hyperbole
Where now the oilfields of ketchup, the acres of hair?
A shame to knock the old place down, they say,
Drifting along, We had some good times here.

old film
Celluloid shades of Garbo, Garland, Groucho, } famous actors/
Welles, Goofy, Wayne, rise hissing in the air, } actresses/cartoons
And Hi-yo! the call sounds high and very far off,   cartoons
Let's go, big fella! Hi-yo, Silver, away!
↳ Lone Ranger used as voice of the crane man

→ poem shows that buildings can hold memories / & building have a stor to tell.
→ link to the past and to old cinema: UAF romanticies the old cinema
→ Highlights the importance of a cinema : Stanza 4 shows how cinema effects style.
=> real cultural images.

Annotations (handwritten):

fanthorpe's need to give a 'voice' to the dispossessed and inarticulate

homeless people in London.

Counting Song

counting the social classes
age groups abt true Londoners.

One man and his dog } refers to
Went to mow a meadow. } country lifestyle

Glamourous image of London

Not always the same dog, — indivs. wu have individuality
But the man looks the same, disposable,
Scrapped. Hungerford Bridge his meadow.

economical use of language : zebras '15s & 17s reflects hectic pace of life.

society   — well known place in London where homeless life

This is the city we come to when we're young,   voice of homeless
With the golden pavements. Where office-workers whisk
Like weir-water over zebras; where 15s and 77s ← zebra crossing & buses
Snuffle down bus lanes, showy as heralds.

Dick wittington

One woman and a baby — shows introduction to a new sector!

cynicisem/humour
Probably borrowed, we say, not looking,
Moving on. We need to move on. passers by are embarrassed
Our shoes are embarrassed. Our shoes are what she sees. — shes ashamed → shes looking at floor.

There's less of sky, now the great Lego thumbs   tall office buildings
Angle their vacant heads into the gullspace, (sky)
But the saints watch us, Martin the beggars' friend, St. martin in field.
Bride in her wedding-cake hat, and Paul,   Paul's Cathedral
Skywise and circumspect, sitting out centuries
Under his helmet, Thames washing past,
Refusing to run softly. — harsh slide of London

being all-seeing

One gran and her bottle } homeless/dispossessed — who have
Have given up on mowing } given up on life.

disposable — not needed =) opposing images
These are waste people, grazing in litterbins, — eating from litter bins
Sleeping in cardboard, swaddled in broadsheets wrapped up
And Waitrose plastic bags, who will not be recycled, reincarnated
Must lie where they fall. — will die and no-1 will care

These are the heirs, the true Londoners,   Fanthorpe faces
Who work in this stern meadow. The others   the reality of life.
Are on their way to somewhere else: |
'normal'/office workers

n Meadow =
don/H. bridge

31

ost-war everything goes back to normal
gives voice of homeless.

a refusion to face up to reality

Statesmen and filmstars, remote, chauffeur-driven;
Volatile journalists, folding themselves in taxis,
As homegoers fold themselves into introspection
And the *Evening Standard*.

Written on Hungerford Bridge in letters of chalk:
Save Our Earth. Save Twyford Down.

Save Earth. Save Twyford Down. Save every one.

Twyford Down, under threat from motorway. Many trees cut down major protests.

THEME: Life is precious? appreciate every second.

* Comparison to life as a poet + prisoner in Death Row.

link to Tyndale in Darkness

Death Row Poets

(for Marie Mulvey Roberts)

a feminist

Career: feeling of being called by God to certain professions

irony — the idea-u cant stop trapped

doesnt + to be — she called to for death watching life pass

To wait, to watch. Vocation
Of the prisoner and the poet.

feeling — God

as if being a poet is an affliction — cant choose not to be

Not those who choose to watch,
Chess-players, crossword-puzzlers, those who flinch

painful

quite meaningful things to pass time = prisoner/poet counts the hours —> does not appreciate life

From the blazing face of Time, and focus — personification — time has a face and name
On small exacting things. But the poets,

lateness   prison sentence/life

The prisoners, whose stretch is finite, — time running out
Look straight in Time's face, and see   undefined stretch

v. imp.

The unrepeatable marvel of each second.
Consider these prisoners, these poets.

who see how positive life is, how worth living, who look forward to things and dont want to miss any opportunity.

same 'job'.

changes become later

Consider also those who are taught not to see, — the pain/suffering/death
To blanket violence by conditioning:

conceal/cover   training   executioners

Decent men, kind to wives, who must not know
Which of them pressed the button; — executioner

5 have to press — dont know who did final act of killing.

practice executions: refusal to look at reality

Who must learn to see the dummy, not the person; — prisoner is a dummy not a person —> keeps conscience clear.
Who must be helped, by rectal plug and catheter,

racked — lose control of bowels — final act of dying is scary/not pleasant, hiding reality

Not to smell the body's final protest.
Consider these men also. And those who give them their orders.

Poets + prisoners linked by enjambement.

criticises those who refuse to see the bigger picture + enjoy life, who hide away from reality or are narrow minded

use of the poet suffering for their art: poetry is a life sentence like being on death row

Poet compares herself to a prisoner + poetry is seen both as an affliction and a gift

33

← CLEAVER

dying from terminal illness

meaning & implication

doctors
PROFESSIONALS — social/care workers

negative, colloquial

The Unprofessionals
— family — dont know what doing
— volunteer nurses — out of love

When the worst thing happens, — dying from a terminal illness

limited time hours
That uproots the future, — uncertainty — of time of death — changes everything
That you must live for every hour of your future,

distant
They come, — family — volunteers? "list of threes"
Unorganized, inarticulate, unprofessional; — negative list. — persuasive device.

sympathy
drink
empathises / reinforces point — v. sad
They come sheepishly, sit with you, holding hands, — SAD!

From tea to tea, from Anadin to Valium, — pain killers — weak to v. s*

make-shift beds
Sleeping on put-you-ups, answering the phone, — get over the counter
Coming in shifts, spontaneously, — obliged to be there. — chore

Talking sometimes, — AWKward
Alliteration
shows routine
About wallflowers, and fishing, and why — simple things in life — bizarre unconnected topics — y death? Y me? — sympathy
—Dealing with Kleenex and kettles, — conveys HELPLESSNESS
Doing the washing up and the shopping, — life goes on — things/jo still need to be do
no change =no hope

Simile
Ref. to Blitz
HELPLESS
—Like civilians in a shelter, under bombardment, — war — against dea
Holding hands and sitting it out — waiting
Through the immortality of all the seconds,
Until the blunting of time. everlasting

the death of person.
Limplyed meaning

Comforting each other

⑤ — Ⓕ change
pre pares us for death

Time is gna carry on → not gna stop even after death

Repetition
* to empathise point — POEM = SAD
* Realistic — comforting each other — LOTS OF EMOTION

* Economical language
portrays lots of emotio

* Poem — all 1 sentence = 1 full stop
* contrast btwn humans + time
* Circular structure — lang EG: rep 'holding hands'
* Poem — a tribute.

A Major Road for Romney Marsh

It is a kingdom, a continent.
Nowhere is like it.

(Ripe for development)

It is salt, solitude, strangeness.
It is ditches, and windcurled sheep.
It is sky over sky after sky.

(It wants hard shoulders, Happy Eaters,
Heavy breathing of HGVs)

It is obstinate hermit trees.
It is small, truculent churches
Huddling under the gale force.

(It wants WCs, Kwiksaves,
Artics, Ind Ests, Jnctns)

It is the Military Canal
Minding its peaceable business,
Between the Levels and the Marsh.

(It wants *investing in roads*,
Sgns syng T'DEN, F'STONE, C'BURY)

It is itself, and different.

(Nt fr lng. Nt fr lng.)

Handwritten annotations:

it was under the sea

inspired by a visit to Romney Marsh

nature VS man's destruction — known as 5th continent
(S) + (E) of royal military canal in Sussex
— research

rich area → salt marsh

It is a kingdom, a continent. — unique

age of bygone age
sibilance (allit.s)
It is salt, solitude, strangeness. — undeveloped land, so it's its own, contrasting voice, wanting to destroy it
It is ditches, and windcurled sheep. — metaphor

natural imagery

personification
connection btwn old & new
It is obstinate hermit trees. — Rhyme scheme
It is small, truculent churches — past → centre of universe
Huddling under the gale force.

★ JUXTOPOSITION
(↳ putting a beautiful england #against our wants & needs
today, modern society)

hostile
church = village
many churches create hostility btwn them

comparing old generation needs to new generation needs

we are now alienated in our homes.

not including the vouls

THEME —
sense of change
past being threatened)
(mm) — wants & needs of modern society.

~~~ — lines — what it has

① — Nature
↳ describing Romney marsh

(~) — as u go down ~ geting more easier and abbreviated.

moral — If we focus on the present 2 much → we rgna lose touch with past ↳ ...struggle btwn past &...

— abt 2 opposing voices)
↳ developer & campaigner

nacce → rushing thru
↳ fast → ... society

middle ages — only rich had access to salt. BT. as society ...

of King Arthur — knights of the round table

DNA — inheritence. — whats being passed on.
(Deoxyribonucleicacid) — genetics!

"... and so their horses went where they would." — refers to the time when
they were all dead
and the horses were free

Malory: *Le Morte d'Arthur* XXI ch x

The death of Arthur

to reflect the passing of time

Arthur =

So at the end the company dissolved. — modern lang — to show how the
past influences us
[kingdom]

Kings died. Queens turned into nuns. — Guinevere

Knights came to grief, or left in symbolic boats. — the magic boat

They made Lancelot a priest. And those other knights

Read holy books, and holp for to sing mass, — round table

And tinkled little bells. Then it was over. — very short sentences = finality

flippant, dismissive! — Medievil lang, dnt now what it means?
— the past comes through
rank represent
the present

Tone = flippant! Dismissive, chatty

Their horses, the noble destriers, — the best ones

like the — The lordly ones, plaited and groomed and oiled, — the best treatment

the weren't — With their grave names and their alarming harness, — they were richly
serious decorated

used for work!! — Who carried nothing, except men to war, — this was all they did
and now they aint got
nothing

to show movement — Stepped mildly over the brambles, tasted grass,

Cantered composedly through the forest waste — it what they did
of before

Of early England, and at last — time passing

They are free but they have retained their sense of nobility — Went where they liked, quick and shining

Through kingdoms. Time whittled them down. — to make smaller
freedom / time passing

They became the dwarfish ponies of now, — wild ponies of Brittian

Shaggy and hungry, living on the edge. — how things change over
past, b

baby horse — little white mark on the forehead.

Sometimes, in a foal's crest, you can see — how they
retain over
the pas

eg. pop idols turning it to us after talking bout the horses — Some long-extinguished breeding. So in us, — like with us!

The high-rise people and the dispossessed, — no house — a brenv kind

The telly idols, fat men in fast cars, — the ordinary people are still

Something sometimes reverts to the fine dangerous strain

Of Galahad the high prince, Lancelot the undefeated,

Arthur the king.

comedy-element

'dore deicl grains' — 1st poem — Romantic Heros

• finds past better
then present.

She believes the good things from the
past still get passed on through the
generations.

A sense of Nobility always survives

Through generations people will change but the
past always lives on through the presence

36

1 Stanza — words symb. death

2–3 — society of K.Arthur compared 2 society
society part, present & future.

Grand Union

In the faintly rocking three foot of the cut
Two grey heads drowse on the permanent double.

Elsewhere, adult children wonder if they're safe,
The dog pines mildly in its boarding kennels.

They are at peace in their clean unchallenging ship,
Enfranchised from garden, telephone and friends,

Next meal a certainty at the Boatman's Arms.

The smutty water oils and clots around them,
Eavesdropping on the past: bargees' thick talk;

Snorting of horses; muffled shout of the woman
About to be raped, as the men close in on her.

Happy, old girl? he asks. *Oh, very happy.*

[Handwritten annotations:]

Two worlds joining together

The present & the past!

emphatic to show they are free to leave everyone behind

boats on canal

Two older people on holiday v. calm & quiet.

its been moored!

— The depth of the canal

old people & napping

double bed or a pun on a double drink?

The roles are reversed. The children are looking after the parents

internal rhyme — They have left the dog in a kennel.

nothing to do easy life!

down!?

routine

famous pub? on the route

light care free

dirty — Break!!

sewage system — Industrial place!

synister tone

past

their accents.

ambiguos!

appears to be very illogical!

could be refering to the old woman or the girl being rapped

personifies the water as it is listening in on the talking

the past!

bringing the two worlds together — the water around the barge is getting thicker — around 'them' the old couple!

famworpe giving a voice to the past — giving this place a voice.

At Swarkestone

— a place 9 miles south of Derby

Scottish Prince who tried to invade England.

It is often said that Bonnie Prince Charlie got as far as Derby in his invasion of 1745. In fact,
he reached Swarkestone, some nine miles further south.'
J.G. Collingwood, *The River Trent*

Bonnie Prince Charlie   *idolising history*

He turned back here. Anyone would. After

the way that we look back on history we don't think about the bad thing only the heroism!

The long romantic journey from the North

colloquialism, sentence is s[hort] + blunt = shows stark real[ity]

To be faced with this. A *so what?* sort of place,

A place that, like a mirror, makes you see.

line of hereditary rule

↑contrast   *incapable of feeling emotion!*

bleak, marsh

A scrubby ridge, impassive river, and beyond,

The flats of Middle England. History waited

the things he wanted

To absorb him. Parliaments, dynasties, empires

list of 3s!

the rest of england

Lay beyond these turnip fields. Not what he wanted.

being consumed in history! — we see him as a character

He could have done it. The German Royals

current royal family

Had packed their bags, there was a run

people were stealing money

funds had accumulated in the bank

On the Bank of England, London stood open as jelly.

Nobody could have stopped him. This place did,

odd image

ie. vulnerable

I wasn't interested in being a ruler being presum[ed] she doesn't k[now]

internal power

one long sentence

And the hurricane that blew his cause from Moidart

In a bluster of kilts and claymores and bright red hair

stereotypical scottish image I humorous

Faded at Swarkestone as they turned their backs,

Withdrawing into battle, slaughter, song.

battle of culloden!

neither town nor country, the nameless masses or 'middle classes'

not real, symbolic of speed, & dramatic power & distruction!

it was a perfect time for him to take over as london was vunarable - like jelly

similly!

noise movement energy

UAF exploring what it could have been about swarkestone th[at] halted Bonnie Prince charlie in his tracks → possibly bcoz of som[e] superstitious or frightning thing. UAF makes swarkestone seem so ordinary

38

Lostwithiel in February

lite but cold!

the towns people!

Civil, unfriendly, they answer
Our questions with a small pause first- *suspisous!*
As if to say *Is this an interrogation?* - *someones voice.*

move clumsily!

We blunder aimlessly round their shops, *not buying anything!*
Exclaiming and moving on. Who wants
Walking sticks, ammonites, books about Daphne du Maurier, *famous novalist from cornwall!*

shell fossils!

3 things typical of cornwall!

This time of year? It takes the huge - *exageration*
Communal chumminess of August to generate
Such off-the-cuff traffic. Here, in a quiet season,

fakeness of friendlyness!

enjoyment slowing the poem down!

We brood on empty chairs in cafes, For Sale signs,
Open at Easter. But it's not just that, *something more*
The unmoneyed half-life of the partitioned year.

the yr is split in 2!

reflects the peace and stillness of the town

It's the unheard, unspoken comments as we pass:
We are their revenue, and so they hate us
For making them what we want. In summer

cornwall relies on tourism!

They will be different, vernacular, picturesque.
Now we can hear the authentic Cornish snarl,
Razor's edge language of the occupied. *wild animal - harsh!*

the atmosphere of the town

sense of resentment and bitterness! They need the tourists coz of the money!

as if something bads gna happen.

an attack on the artificality on the places that are based on tourism! Its only there for the tourists

war time - invasion a war btwn the resisdence & tourests!

the people are only complete for 1/2 their life

talking in dialect - culture

Greensted Church

Stone has a turn for speech.
Felled wood is silent
As mown grass at mid-day.

These sliced downright baulks
Still wear the scabbed bark
Of unconquered Epping
Though now they shore up
Stone, brick, glass, gutter
Instead of leaf or thrush.

Processing pilgrims,
The marvels that drew them —
Headless king, holy wolf —
Have all fined down to
Postcards, a guidebook,
Mattins on Sunday.

So old, it remembers
The people praying
Outside in the rain
Like football crowds. So old
Its priests flaunted tonsures
As if they were war-cries.

Odd, fugitive, like
A river's headwaters
Sliding a desultory
Course into history.

Handwritten annotations:

link to DNA, Room where everyone goes

wood has now been replaced with new materials such as these... Like trees chopped down / cut wood

past has been silenced.
sym – old b death of woods (trees)

a new exterior has been build 2 protect the wooden walls

Personifying the building

Stone has a turn for speech. – The stone is on the outside
Felled wood is silent – The wood is on the inside
– The modern has silenced the past

The roughly squared pillars of wood.
timber beam for building
very rough.
Personification of the bank
negative

forrest!
hold up
Their purpose is to hold up the church

in the previous 'life' they wld be there for the birds & leaves!

reinforces that it was a rough w[ood] constructed that have lasted all this time.

felled the wood has been it no longer has leaves etc / it holds new materials

alliteration / adds to sense of conveyer belt

cynical tone

to refer to something from the past
religious vocab

become touristy
The history of the church and is popularity has led it 2 become a tourist attraction & the production of tacky goods.
commenting on how outdated religion has become
morning prayers.

Replace our relig[ious] needs

The church can remember up to medieval times

wooden church
past & the present
replaced by material world of sport

material is our new religion

shaved heads
(religious, practical reasons, age
came in crowds to
pray. Religion was popular. Whatever the weather, pple went to pilgrimage — devotion

link 2 'Room where every[one] goes
cleanliness –
diff cultures shave heads

hiding from something / or running away?

Streams Flowing from the source of a river
half hearted / superficial way

childhood old age – hair fall[ing] out

Full rhyme – unusual for Fanthorpe

the little wooden church hidding in the modern exterior & its being forgotten

she is trying to bring this history back

Personification: gives the church life / a personality.

40

Helpston

This is where it happened. These are the fields,
Plain, with a Gothic augmentation of hedge.
These are the skies, high, hard, dispensing light.
The modern contributions: tight-lipped housing;
Trees pruned to the bone, leafless as winter;
The church bell's funereal bark as it deals out time.

A banshee plane roughs our hair. A detached native
Tells where you're buried. This is where
You wanted to be, what you loved. We came

Because of you. The wind comes at us,
Swearing, along the furrows.

[Handwritten annotations:]

Dedication to John Clare the poet!

born in Helpston

did farmyard jobs — thresher, Bird scarer, farm Labourer

J.C's birth / abt his life / death

design/style — Grand → man's manipulation of the country side

something thats been added to. → changed

harsh stressed alliteration — light thru clouds

Personification

no real sense of community!

series of images — i.e black image! he doesn't really care about John Clare

death (the bells ringing):

mad-woman noise

bad sound - ref to death

enjambment

tells abt passing of time

wind

clare! its important to her

flying low!

the harsh reality of the place!

idea of trying to control nature

when u plow the earth

what is allowed

seeds

Sadness! people like clare aren't remembered the way way he shld be!

41

consonence - alliteration of the first vowel
The only poem in the anthology
that has Rhythm Rhyme
pace = faster! - steady Rhythmic beat!
* Rhym couple ALL way thru

Under the Motorway

The beat makes it sound like a nursery rhyme

Flashy sporty car

There they go charging through the muck,
Lada, Lagonda and Leyland truck.
But under the motorway, what's there?
What lies in wait? Is it brown and bare
Like earth in fields? Is it rocks and stones?
Is it dead people, and dinosaurs' bones?

Something no doubt of all of these.
But more importantly, it's seeds
Waiting their time to spring to the top
When the tarmac ends and the lorries stop.
When there is no more Renault and Rover,
Roads will be thick with Cleavers and Clover.

Petrol and diesel will both dry up
But that doesn't happen to a Buttercup.
Flowers shoot upwards with mighty heaves
And sprout in a flurry of stems and leaves.
Here they come shouldering through the road,
Willowherb, Woodruff, Woundwort, Woad.

On viaduct, bypass, clearway, trunk,
Mercedes, Minis turn to junk.
But Love-in-a-Mist and Love-lies-Bleeding —
They're on our side, and they're succeeding.
Rolls Royce and Volvo, their day is done,
But Charlock and Dandelion blaze in the sun.

(handwritten annotations:)
Alliteration — (consonance)
questions, uncertainty!
tries to question & answer
giving examples of the flowers
rhyming couplet — full Rhyme — cars — ababab
rhythmical qu = childlike curiosity — childs wonder
childlike rhyme — old b seen as a — sound like modern society — lives here — the past - history — prehistorical — era lasting life — the cycle of life
brand of cars
flowers
alliteration consonance — capital letter - importance status
nature flower
strenght / power
time lapse photography
speed movement
alliteration consonance — bordging
different types of roads
harsh sounding
minies have rolled
contrast the soft sounding names
powerful word
yellow — power & strenght as if it were the sun!
flowess. idea of burning
strenght good against the odds
nature doing good against the odds
society (manmade) will crumble eventually
market need resentretion childs

She is saying that our material things wont be here forever but nature will be!

42   The full Rhyme- saying that she is certain that nature will last years!
reflets - nature
* only poem using PROnounced rhyme/rhythm structure.

What, in our house?

> "The play *(Macbeth)* is remarkably short, and it may be there has been some cutting."
> J.G. Collingwood

Macduff   O Banquo, Banquo,
    Our royal master's murdered.
Lady Macbeth   Woe, alas!
    What, in our house?
Banquo   Too cruel anywhere.
Lady Macbeth   That's not the point. Who cares for anywhere?
    Mere woolly-minded liberals. But *here*
    Is where I am, my house, my place, my world,
    My fortress against time and dirt and things.
    Here I deploy my garrison of soap,
    And, like all housewives, just about contrive
    To outmanoeuvre chaos. Not a job
    For men. What man alive will grovel
    Scrubbing at floorboards to mop up the blood?
    (No doubt there's blood? Or if not, sick or shit
    Or other filth that women have to handle?)
Banquo   O gentle lady ...
Lady Macbeth   Only women know
    The quantity of blood there is that waits
    To flood from bodies; how it soaks and seeps
    In wood and wool and walls, and stains for ever.
    No disinfectant, I can tell you, Banquo,
    So strong as blood. Then, the implicit slur
    Upon my hospitality. Was Duncan
    Suffocated? Something wrong with the pillows!
    Was his throat cut? Check the carving knives!
    Poison? Blame the cuisine. I wish to heaven,
    Banquo, he'd died in *your* house. Your wife
    Would tell you how I feel.

Enter Malcolm and Donalbain

Donalbain   What is amiss?
Macduff   Your royal father's murdered.
Malcolm   O, by whom?

43

Lady Macbeth

Such donnish syntax at so grave a moment!
How hard to frame the first and random thought
Detection snuffs at, to seem innocent
And psycholinguistically correct at once)
And my *best* bedroom, too.

Annotations:

- Juxtaposition — comparison of her char, b4 nc now = DIFF.

learned person

word order in sentences.

comment on his respon

v. intelligant lady

sentence to logical for her

structure related to thought
idea, that we say dont reflect how we feel

cant think
no since

• In poem — (F) expresses wit + humour

↳ Adding own scene in Macbeth in a random way

has a moment on intellect
↓
then goes ble
(into 'sterotypical woman)
↓
abt clenliness.

Says she harnt got the lang 2 express wa shes really saying — words dont reflect feelings
↓
her innocent of being a woman
↓
= expresses thru womans 'things'

expression of being a woman

- uses comic conventions to make drastic + comic points
- Diff to other poems — form of a play
- title — links bk to 'Safe as house'.
- Comedy btwn poems 43/45

44

[handwritten: type of a mountine hardness of climbing!]

*[handwritten: * very long poem]*

[handwritten: Virginia wolf & father Sir Lesley Stevenston]

An easy day for a lady

[handwritten: narratives]

1. THE CLIMBER *[handwritten: — mountinevring]*

The Alps were right for him. Unpeopled. Snow
Affirmed no one had ever been that way.
Melchior, his honest guide, tactfully keeping
Out of sight; his Cambridge friend,
Kennedy, Taylor, some gentlemanly cleric,
Don, civil servant, slogging a long way after,
But sure to hail him at last with that fierce reliable
Cambridge facetiousness able men use.

[handwritten: deserted]

[handwritten: important to be first & to do things no one else has done - childish]

A clean, competitive world. The great white heads
Scale one above the other, brow by brow exposing
New challenges, new hazards, a new route,
Like men from another college, suddenly known
As serious rivals for a serious prize.
As candidates are measured by degrees
(Wrangler to passman), so climbs are graded:
Inaccessible; most difficult point in the Alps;
A good hard climb, but nothing out of the way;
A perfectly straightforward bit of work;
An easy day for a lady. *[handwritten: sexist comment]*

She watches him. She will use this later. *[handwritten: - in her writing — very observant]*

[handwritten: contrast between him &]

2. THE FATHER *[handwritten: wrapped in his own world.]*

[handwritten: crap father!]

He's grounded now in a rented Cornish garden,
Stamping his Mr Carter boots over unremarkable
Borders and beds, with children bundling
In and out of the kitchen garden, cricket lawn,
Coffee garden, love garden, endless gardens,
Boxed in by hedges, cheeping everywhere
(One his, three hers, four theirs), so many
Expensive expanding mouths.

[handwritten: all they are = mouths to feed]

45

He bucks himself up with the litany
Of his Alpine firsts: Bietschhorn, Oberaarhorn,
Schreckhorn, Blümlisalphorn, Monte Disgrazia.
Then there's the work in hand, the great Biographies,
Gauging how many lines each life is worth.
Sometimes he's audible. His headful of fossil verse
Suddenly sprouts through the escallonia:
Beware the pine-tree's withered branch! Beware
The awful avalanche! Embarrassing;
But worse the sheer-drop silences in front of strangers.
Like a hole in the world.

She watches him. She will use this later.

[handwritten: ←emphases her role! she looks up 2 him]

3. *THE HEIR*

[handwritten: writing = fame]

[handwritten: inheireted the gift for making mountines from her licurature]

The heir isn't always apparent. All those fine
Upstanding boys, with their Cambridge brains; not them? *[handwritten: ↓]*
The older sisters, Stella, Laura, the Saint?
Not them, not them, but Billy the giddy goat. *[handwritten: comparin him who he - explore mountines she - explores licurature]*
She was the one to inherit the gift
And miss the education. She climbed, unsupervised,
Creating routes, perspectives, sentences,
Climbing above streets, buses, rooms, to take it all in.

[handwritten: she wants to share world with everyone]

He bagged the view at the top. Had to be first.
Wanted it to himself. Below, cosmopolitan cockneys —
Magnifique! Wunderschön! Simply splendid! — suburban cooings
Made Alpine sunsets stink of Baedeker.
But Billy the goat, she capered where he had trampled.
She risked the lunatic leap between feeling and sense,
And invented a syntax for it. She charted
Innominate peaks of silence, emptiness, space;
Shared what she found with all who cared to come.
When time ran out, she walked to death, prospecting

46

The weedy channelled Ouse, that lowland stream,
Stones in her pocket.

She watches this. Some things are never used.

[handwritten annotation: She commited suicide by putting stones in her pocket and walking into a stream.]

An Easy Day for a Lady: Notes

He: Sir Leslie Stephen, famous mountaineer and first editor of the Dictionary of National Biography.

She: His younger daughter, Virginia, who became Virginia Woolf.

Rented Cornish garden: of Talland House, St Ives, celebrated in *To the Lighthouse*. Her father's boots are also immortalised in this novel, but I found Mr Carter's name in Sir Leslie's mountaineering writing.

The Saint: Vanessa (Bell). This was her family nickname, as Billy was Virginia's.

Some things are never used: Virginia Woolf wrote about most things, but not her own death.

Odysseus' Cat

(for Barbara Britton)

> Aged and broken, prostrate on the ground,
> Neglected Argus lies, once fabled hound.
> Odysseus's footsteps he alone descries,
> Perceives the master through the slave's disguise;
> He lifts his head, and wags his tail, and dies.
> *The Corgiad*, trans. J.G.Collingwood.

Not that I don't believe
The first part of the yarn — the ten years' war.
Ten seems quite modest for a genocide.
No, it's the ten years' journey afterwards
I boggle at, bearing in mind
The undemanding nature of the route.
Why did he take so long? One thing's for sure —
Those junkies, cannibals, one-eyed aliens,
And friendly ladies living alone on islands
Well, what do you think? Of course. Exactly.
In the meantime, in another part of the archipelago,
Old Argus had been catsmeat long before.
Man's best wears out, with rushing around and barking,
And digging and wagging. Cats, on the contrary, last:
The harmonious posture, exact napping,
Judicious absences from home... I had, of course,
Been busy. Did what I could to discourage
The mistress's unappealing Don Juans,
Lurked boldly in dark corners, slashing
Shins of passers-by; performed
Uninhibited glissades down dinner tables,
Scattering wine and olives; free fell
From rafters upon undefended necks;
Produced well-timed vomit in my lady's chamber
When a gallant went too far; and I helped
With demolishing the tapestry each night,
Having an inbred talent.

48

<!-- Handwritten annotations present on page include: -->
<!-- "Narrative — dramatic Monologue VOICE — women — CAT" -->
<!-- "greek hero fighting in 10yrs trojan war" -->
<!-- "famed for the 10yr journey to get back to Ithica..." -->
<!-- "he didn't have a cat he had a dog" -->
<!-- "The dog was the only one who knows it him" -->
<!-- "maybe he was unfaithful to his wife?" -->
<!-- "flippant tone / the cat..." -->
<!-- "history is a story - Ref - trojan greek" -->
<!-- "mass killing" (genocide) -->
<!-- "astonished" (boggle) -->
<!-- "coloqueal lang" / "contempry lang" -->
<!-- "She tells the story in a down to earth way - from a womans/cats point of view. Story has been told heroicy from a mans p.o.v!" -->
<!-- "She is challenging him." -->
<!-- "short and conversational / punchy direct conversation" -->
<!-- "Man see women as weak as weariness Heroic / women see weak as Heroic" -->
<!-- "immorality / rotten war / challenging the traditional" -->
<!-- "catsmeat" / "Half - Rhym" -->
<!-- "Tone changes - cats more calm, posh" / "cat war - women" -->
<!-- "women take their time & dnt rush around, like the cat —" -->
<!-- "dog" -->
<!-- "the suiters / lover boy / making a connection CAT to recent history" -->
<!-- "his wife Panelope" -->
<!-- "mechtar again? focus / ALLITERATION" -->
<!-- "well timed humour" -->
<!-- "oxymoron can't LURK boldly only quietly" -->
<!-- "mode of thread - cat picking at yarn" / "women r knitters - make tappist" -->
<!-- "whole thing" -->
<!-- "boastful cats more fen redstron" -->
<!-- "critical term" -->
<!-- "accuratly discribing what went on in odysseus's household while he was away" -->

the cat can get its
own way, like women
Buttering the man:
up oren asking
for something.

feminine
charms →

BOTH?
Odysseus? / Dog?
Rep. each other

So when Odysseus came, I rubbed his legs.
He recognised me — well, he said *Puss, puss,*
Which is all you learn to expect.
                    And then the liar
Concocts this monstrous calumny of me:
He leaves me out, supplants me with a dog,
A dead dog, too. And the one thing
Everyone believes is that dog's tale,
Tale of the faithful hound.
                    You'll see
I've improved his version; cut out the lies,
The sex, the violence. Poor old Argus
Wouldn't have known the difference. But cats
Are civilised. I thought you'd see it my way.

the position
of women
her role is
to simply
please her
husband

play on words

women

TRUTH

rewriting History
History has many versions

The women wld neva go to war!
"If the mothers were in charge there wld
neva be wars because they wld not want
                    their children killed.

feminist joke! — play on words.

mankind - shld be - humankind

dogsmeat - changed 2 - catsmeat!

- thats why women live
longer than men.

TONE
• flippant

what the poem shows!
* challenges the idealised views of history
* shows Fanthorpe interest into the ordinary
and unremarkable (the cat)!
* Presents history in a series of stories that
can be challenged.
49 * Presents a personality of the cat + Fanthorpe's feminist
                                    view
                ↓ pronoun + extra view point.
* she likes dramatic monologues
* Humanises cat - give voice

He refuses to read his public's favourite poem

'I think Yeats hated all his early poems, and 'Innisfree' most of all. One evening I begged him to read it. A look of tortured irritation came into his face and continued there until the reading was over'
Dorothy Wellesley

They always asked for it. He knew they would.
They knew it off by heart: a b, a b,
Reliable rhymes; thoughts they could understand.
But dreams, as well. Their own, their Innisfree.

So why refuse? He knew the rest were better,
His serious bid for immortality.
What man defends the tenets of his twenties?
Who would be tied for life to Innisfree?

"Give us *Arise and go* in your Irish accent,
Give us the cabin, the glade, the beans, the bees.
Not Maud, Byzantium, Crazy Jane, Cuchulain.
We are your public. Give us more Innisfrees."

"A poem heard twelve times in public is dead and finished."
"Ah no! Too much of a good thing there cannot be.
Too much of Shakespeare, Wordsworth, Milton, Shelley,
There is. But not enough of Innisfree.

I will arise and go now — Senator, please! "
"I won't. I can't. I'm not him any more.
Young fool who prattles of crickets and wattles and linnets —
I hate him in the deep heart's core."

50

Deus v. Adam and Another

[handwritten: Eve] *[handwritten: a battle – set out like a court case]*

Summing up for the defence, m'lud, I must say *[handwritten: thoughts]*
(In spite of my learned friend's eloquence)
I see no case to answer. Consider first
The object of the alleged theft. We have no means
Of identifying it. We may, I think, *[handwritten: personal pronoun – direct appeal]*
Safely surmise that it has been consumed. *[handwritten: apple eaten]*
But by whom? I submit, m'lud,
That there is no evidence. Posterity *[handwritten: bin eaten]*
Is going to affirm it was an apple;
The document in the case refers to *fruit*.
The accused are vague: she says it was a lemon; *[handwritten: sour – bad taste – bad things]* *[handwritten: HUMOUR]* *[handwritten: blame rational after things go wrong.]*
He thinks on the whole a raspberry. *[handwritten: nonononono → aloud.]*
A strange case of pilfering we have here: *[handwritten: stealing]*
It's claimed they ate it, but they don't know what it was.

Now the witness. *[handwritten: SATAN/DEVIL]* Members of the jury, *[handwritten: court case]*
What can one say of a witness who, it's alleged,
While the offence was being committed, had the normal *[handwritten: 4 limbs ⇒ abnormal]*
(Four) number of limbs, and an inadequate, nay, a persuasive *[handwritten: talked eve into eating apple]*
Voice with which it addressed the female accused,
Yet which now appears in court literally legless, *[handwritten: Drunk – snake → putting down witness]*
And proverbially struck dumb, so that it can only *[handwritten: unreliable]*
Hiss and wriggle apologetically? M'lud and members of the jury,
It is quite clear, is it not, that the serpent has been got at?
I will not exceed my brief and suggest by whom, *[handwritten: By God]*
But we are all men of the world, are we not, *[handwritten: Good vs Evil]*
Members of the jury (except, of course, for those of us
Who are women)? *[handwritten: sexist joke – idea sexism passed down over time.]*

Lastly, m'lud, the very peculiar *[handwritten: markers]* *[handwritten: God]*
Question of motive. The accused had been warned,
As you have heard, by the landlord, not to eat
The fruit of the tree of knowledge of good and evil;
If they did, they would die. This, m'lud,
We call a penalty clause. It is claimed they *did* eat,
Whatever it was, apple, lemon, or good red herring,
But didn't die. For here they are in court,

[handwritten: didn't die physically ↓ became moral ↓ died on a spiritual level]

Mr Adam and Mrs Eve. So did they break the clause?
I see no evidence. The prosecution fail
To establish a theft. The only witness —can't rely on serpant to tell truth
Has been tampered with. And finally,
Do the defendants look as though knowledge of good and evil
Had come their way? Their rather pathetic ensemble —formal
Of verdure hardly suggests it. Would such knowledge
Result in so trifling a step forward —eg fig leaves
As covering one's private parts? O no, members of the jury.
If we knew good from evil, we would know the answers *Saying
To the perennial hard questions — abortion, pacifism, Humanity can
The rights of trees, euthanasia, what-about-Europe. understand
Do our two defendants, shivering there in the dock, themselves.
Look like creatures able to conceptualize such questions,
Let alone answer them? M'lud, I rest my case.

* Uses a comic court case ~~to took~~ as a vehicle to ...
   explore a serious thing→ what humanity is really abt.
                                                  ↓
                                            Adem + Eve.

* V. formal structure/lang.

* V. logical Perspective — God vs Devil

* Puts down women

* Not based on logic — A + E dno evn wa they ate.

52

THEME ② (F) + Degas r similar, bcoz
she wants to show the
reality of life

on surface is aironing women
↳ beneath - voice of woman tlking
abt man painting her pic
↳ putting a slant on our
expectations

gossip/pronoun

The voice

Woman Ironing* — Dramatic monologue

confidential tone/ v. chatty

surprises reader / unusual
across a crowded
room → PUN!

I thought I knew what was coming when he said — LIE
He wanted to do my likeness at the ironing.
I live in the city, people tell you things. Me looking at him,
It would be, across the ironing board, my hair and my eyes
In a good light, and something a bit off the shoulder.

smouldering sensuality
a sexual expectation
shows rep. of ironers

short sentence - abrupt - anti-climax
all an illusion
numerous colloquial

But it wasn't. He rushed around drawing curtains.
Made it hard to iron. O yes, I had to keep ironing.
He needed to see the strength, he said. Kept on
About my dynamic right shoulder, then left it out,
Though you can see where he ought to have put it.

she knows the terminology - critical of art
UAF giving voice to masses - to ironing lady

Come on, what's-your-name, he kept saying, — ITALICS - narrator changes
Show us that muscle-power! That's what I'm after. — 2nd voice
I might've been an engine, not a person. — her thoughts / no respect / colloquial / chatty
No, I didn't take to him. I'm used to rudeness.
But he was making such a sketch of me. — comedy joke / drawing/fool (PUN)

didn't fall in ♡ wid client

④ challenges his painting of her when she irons
his class/status - imp.

If someone's paying you, it isn't easy
To speak your mind. Still, Sir, I said,
I really don't want to see my hair like that — womans personality/voice
All scraped back, like a hot person's hair, — muscular, scruffy
And anyone can tell that under my arms I'm sweating. — replace with "sex".

Hair? Sweat? That's how it is when you iron, — mans personality
Says he. *You're not here to tell me what to do.*
I'll make you permanent, the way you look — The Reality
When you're ironing. O yes, he says, I'll show you — She was dependent on £ of man
The way you look when no one's watching.

idea of portraying REAL women

prostitution can b cn as a casual activity

*Note: The original title of this painting is La Repasseuse. The Walker Art Gallery translates this as *Woman Ironing*, which suggests to me a casual activity, like woman smiling. I'd think it more accurate if the painting were known as *Ironing Woman*. Degas's ironers are trained specialists.

AF makes us sympathetic/empathise with woman
AF takes ordinary pple + gives them a voice ∴ she captures their
views + ideas → expresses her views on everything.

53

↳ by giving sym1 a voice - ur making them sumink
⇒ giving them a history

compare to: He refuses to read his publics fav. poem, Odysseus Cat
Pg 50   PG. 48

Annotations (handwritten): Fanthorpe is criticising people for thinking poetry is too hard!

Painter and Poet
← a warning against poets

contrasting them

HEROIC — *like a lesson – patronising tone*

allowing tones + colour to merge – jargon of art

* Painters are self-obsessed

Watch the painter, children.
The painter is painting himself.
Palette enfisted, aloft; brush brandished. *– showy – alliteration*
There are men watching the painter painting, *making the language of painters*

ppl pay £ to see painting

Children. The spectacled one with a beard *v.people wanting*

UAF's commentary on capitalism

Is saying *Magnificent! a touch of sfumato there!*
Did you see how he gouached that bit of scumble? *2nd VOICE = painter*
O, a very good investment, gentleman. *You can't go wrong,*
Financially speaking, when the artist has used – The artist technique

people want to see paintings

So much technique. There! did you see how he stippled? *compared to the poets technique*
My advice is, certainly purchase. Always a market *draw using dots*
For work of this kind. The painter listens, children,
And smiles a banker's smile. He does
A spot more impasting. *knows his work is immediately profitable – process of laying on paint thickly – ironic*

not likes it → doesn't receive $ for being poet. poet is being ironic

* shows that ppl have become lazy! i.e. they prefer the visuals more!

VERY DULL Now, children, the poet. He is less exciting.
implies no imp. All he brandishes is a ball-point, *near lag*
Which he plays with on unastonishing paper. *playing with word order*

people dnt care about poetry

See him unload his disorganised wordhoard, *lonely/boring*
Children, as he sits alone. No one comes *his technique is almost feared by the children!*
To admire, or commission. Having only
Himself to please, he tinkers at pleasing himself.
Watch silently now as that metaphor *sarcastic*
Fans slowly out, like a fin from the sea. *humour – describing his use of metaphors with a simile*

implies his work benefits no1 else

Did you notice him then, secret and shy as an otter, *clever of*
Transferring an epithet? See that artless adverb *portrayed in neg way*

useless!

Mutate into a pun! And now — O children, *UAF is describing her own job*
Keep very quiet — he is inserting a verb!) *as opposed to painting* ** Doesn't g voice to poet less imp*

sarcastic tone

A cryptic cipher, for friends' eyes only, he splices
Into his work, not guessing that what he writes *not everyone understands the reasons for the way the poem is written!*
Will turn into a *text*, a *set text*, – *reference to Shakespeare*
Children; nor that you will think
He committed it deliberately to hurt you.

Shakespeare? – poet?

The children who have to study

Invest in the painter, children; as for the poet, him! *– have to endure boring long ta of studying*
Bad luck is catching. I should steer clear. *like a careers talk*

→ *comical poem: poet making 'fun' of her job = explaining what it's like to be a poet compared to a painter which seems easy ↔ implies poetry has a deeper sig. – have to look beneath the surface to understand it.*

54

→ Poet is seen as a v. lonely figure – writing only for themselves.

→ Did UAF know her work was GCSE/A'level set text when she wrote the poem?

publishers imprint or emblem!
'the sign of the publisher

Colophon — poem about the business of publishing. and the history.

'We're not going out of the book business, we're just throwing away the paper and the print
... Books won't disappear, they'll just become marginalised.'
(Peter Kindersley, of Dorling Kindersley) - *printed books becoming less relevant!*

Led by *Exchange and Mart* we came to Slough:- *she goes to buy*
A nest of garages, a leaking roof, *a printing press!*
Rain spitting into plastic buckets. Man *very ordinary thing!*
In overalls, cloth-capped; a Berkshire voice.

a very ordinary place. run down but extraordinary

the machines
Come up the M4, didjer? Lovely job. *The v. extraordinary*
The great gaunt things loom round him patiently, *thing > comes from a ordinary place*
Hoping for work. *They* come here from all over. *human characteristics to the machines.*
Ipswich. And Leeds. There's several comes from Leeds.

he's 1 person + negative!

They aint being used
the print
How dangerous they were, the ancestors, — *fanthorpe doesn't understand how*
Whose children stand here, endlessly resold, *they can just sit there*
Iron feet in puddles; whose work was burned, *slaves*
Chained, or inherited, precious as manors. *Tyndale!*
powerful but!

the children being sold! slaves!

The printer's devils worked them, skinny, short-lived, *short lives*
Coughing up blood like Keats; and the journeymen, *died of tuberculosis.*
With their mirror-image eyes, masonic alphabet *lived a tragic life*
Beginning ampersand k; ending at r; *jargon! person of low status*
type of font.

the boys who worked the printing presses

Who knew how to handle f, with its double *detail on fonts!*
Delicate kerns; for whom every speck and nick *no craftmanship!*
Had to be right. *Founts over here*, he says. *fountain*
Plantin, yerse. And *Perpetua*. Lovely *Perpetua*. *pun*
fountains type of flowers

no detail no print!

We get what we came for. Come away *list of 3* *he is talking about his garden!*
With a great gape of loss, like losing one's language.
Tigers, elm trees, Perpetua, lovely Perpetua, *doesn't care things that are lost!*
Sidling into extinction. No more, yerse. *listing*

damn *printing press* *press* *things that are lost*

We paid. He slotted the flatbed into the boot.
There you go. Cheers, lifting a hand as we left.
It felt like a blessing. Could be. We needed one.
He seemed like a man who had the power to bless.

in italian means last forever

personal pronoun *They had the power to publish.*

55

The man represents the lack of appreciation of our cultural past.

other topic

A DRAG QUEEN! GAY.

Queening It — FAKING IT

Graham Norton queens it!

Inside every man there lurks the Widow Twankey,
Brazen and bosomed as a figurehead,
Dressed to the tens,
Lusting to get out,

Lusting for the frou-frous and the pads,
For the wig like a fierce self-raising pudding,
For the Cupid's bow visible over a measured mile,
For the slit skirt, the rangy shaven legs,
The Pennine heels.

Snatching those parts the girls aren't really up to —
The Ladies Bracknell, Thatcher, Macbeth;
Imogen, Rosalind,
(Written for chaps, after all).

How she holds her audience, the Widow!
The men, because she knows what they like;
And the women, sitting relaxed inside their stretchmarks,
Plugged in to their PMT and their HRT,
Their caesareans and their hysterectomies,
Their design faults, poor dears, glad to be made to laugh,
Not caring about the half-shrugged message,
This is how it's done, admiring her dash,
As the monstrous lashes flick, the colossal cleavage throbs.

These are the women men like. Not the supermarket
Slowlane crawlers, near tears, running out of cash;
Tired, with sneezing kids, in endless surgeries;

Not the women we run to in trouble, fat
Putters-on of kettles, who listen, and wait,
And hug if we want it, and are still wearing slippers;

Not the uncertain people, stared at in streets,
For whom both *Gents* and *Ladies* present problems;
Who practise belonging somewhere, but never do.

56

How expert, admired is Twankey, modulating midway tones,
Making the best of both sexes, the true Queen of Hearts!

The way a person shld be is inbetween man & women .

But we who must wear our true hearts on our sleeve —
How to do that? Tell us the answer, Widow,
If you know.

have it all.

1) challenges the idea of gender sterotypes
   The American form of femmism - everyone is equal
2) people are not what they seem - they are always
                              acting or playing
                                   a role
3) she challenges our sexuality.

— pantomine dame - always be a man.

* Juxdpidition - see man as a maitronly character
↳ eg - BOOBS=MILK   dressed up as WOMEN
                         = get a motherly
                              fig

57

*Poem celebrates water as a religion.

RELIGIOUS

Comic humour - black comedy

*comparing religion + water

- Double extended metaphor →clever

*symbolic-critical modern people

Water everywhere

everybody

many gods

Officially they do not acknowledge this god. → water religion in - The god general we wo

Officially they honour (assorted) immortals

In stone buildings with pioneering roofs. spires, pioneering, tusky (domes)

hot water

'safe as houses' → contrast to title

Their houses betray them. Above ceilings,

water

humour

Tanks for the precious stuff. Below, a shrine toilet = water = worship pla

To the godhead. Here they may stand alone (tap) religious imagery

↳bathroom

shower   bath

(In confessional boxes,) or lie full length)

singing in bath

humor

In his hollow bed, singing. Here he sometimes speaks

In loud, disquieting, oracular tones. high rhetoric

com ima

live in water - holy

└ when tap is turned on ↳ gurgling noise it makes

symbolic/

Fish are considered holy; where they go

personel?

We found contemplatives, with green umbrellas, people who think = fishermen

Making symbolic gestures at the stream.

act of fishing.

make ground holy using water

In the hot month they consecrate their gardens

wash the car

With a wet (rite) involving children, rubber, dogs. hose pipe sprinkle puddle...

On Sunday mornings they lustrate the car. ritual prayer - rite

religious / pagans - BU religion wash purify with water old old cliché

They pretend to disparage the god and his rainy gift, entise

Using set (litanies) *Lovely weather for ducks!* They refuse to make it duck

Last Thursday we had our summer. Flaming June! negative

lang from the church

(Black comedy is native to this people). old fashioned joke about rain

negative + sarcastic   2nd voice   british   belongs?

pun <dam!

weather men

Daylong, nightlong, ministers of the god religion boiling hot gives weather in

Recite on different airways his moods and intentions. forecast

like priest of religion = water

The people claim not to believe. But they listen. The weather

I can't trust the weatherman = wrong truth

critique ppl - don't appreciate good literature

Their literature is great. They never read it.

TONE

Water, water everywhere the only - the weather man title

Line they can quote, Though ignorant of the context,

They reckon these words cover everything.

Rome of the ancient marines (by Samual Taylor) colerridge

we talk wi for granted personified H2O - religion

THEMES /IDEAS

*water is valuable + we take it for granted + don't appreciate it - water is a metaphor for lit. which we don't appreciate

* uses 58 religious imagery to show importance of water

Damage Limitation

Barbaric, unruly, alarming,
The power of those who would rather not;

Who, while the others are chewing or snoring
Or pondering duty-free,
Sustain, by a massive exertion of will
The whole company in air;

Or who avert their magic eyes
From small useful shops in marginal districts,
Since if they look, the next message will be
Closing Down Sale and *Everything Must Go;*

Like the man whose son was riding
The Derby favourite. Family watched downstairs,
But he ran a bath, laid his dangerous
Body in it, earthed it in water,
Made himself harmless;

And those spires, that hover and start
To waver in air when the wrong eyes look.
Safer the country parish with its twice-a-year congregation
Whose harvest offerings come to church privately
And after dark: dogged, peculiar, warm.

59

annotations (handwritten):
* alot Fanthorpes Dad — bcoz lesbian — dad stops talking 2 her
[maybe what she wishes. — rshp with dad.] disinherited by fath
. little girl — she goes looking for worms for fishing bate
lucky — faith

On Worms, and Being Lucky

semi-autobiographical — the relationship with her dad.

Rep. father
solid/strong
childhood
↓ b4 lesbian
idea of perfect beach image
lift up

Two kinds of sand. One heavy, gritty,
That falters moodily under your toes, like custard;
The other, shiny weedy ribs, and further, — enjambement
other kid? stranger fetched less solid - after

Out of sight, the standstill sea. You tramp along
In sunbonnet and spade, summer's regalia.
You choose a grey snake's nest, slice into it,

in sand - looks poo. like dog. need for fishing

And yes, there *are* lugworms, and you carve them out,
And he hoicks you up, your dad, to the space round his head.
You've got the knack, my princess, he says. *You're lucky.*

complicated rshp
her-child
ALLITERATION
understand each other
DAD — feel special

BETTING
personal pronoun

Then there's your turn for betting. Bored by favourites,
You always picked the unfancied outsider.
The field foundered at Becher's. Or something.
picking the best horse

lucky / horse ran | hes luck = knack finding lugworm

Dad

Anyway, yours won, against the odds
(*Lucky, my princess!*) since you knew it would,
And knew it into winning (*Sweetheart. Lucky.*)
(fate) 'magic eyes' → she wanted it 2 won so it won.

time shift (F) or Sis

After the operation, you were sent for.
(He was propped up in bed, reeking of ether,
Possibly dying.) You held the big limp hands,
possibly she is dieing
pain killer
grow old - image of him helpless
teenage pulled

lugworms

And lugged him back to life, like a cow from a bog.
He clung to your luck, and kept it
For two more years. You gave him something,
Not knowing what it was. (*The knack*, he wheezes.)
back from death
keep him alive
stanzas 5 & 6
HOPE
* get sense narrator is an outsi...

think - was it just love?

Or love, maybe. Two kinds of luck.
My luck, dear father, flashy and absurd,
A matter of long odds and stop-press news;
only time calls 'my'

how he changed her life with his optimism

Yours was the gift that sees life gold side up,
So that a knack of finding worms becomes
A serious blessing. — links whole poem together

dads new —
his optimising was the real luck!

• written in 3rd person
• @ talking abt sister's rship with 60 fathe
  — or her wish 4 her rship wid dad

annotations (top):
v. deep poem - sounds diff from a (T) poem as it is all abt extended daffodils

bargny at religion and is saying religion is not the exact science

person who has reverence coll or

Daffodil Ministry

not in typical (T) poem

Rep: hope — harsh sounds - reflect her anger

One of the more difficult denominations. — peeps who give false talks
No artless formula of psalm, collect,
And-now-to-God-the-father: unrelenting ministry—
Of the solo conscience. Mankind's cheerless concerns
Can drop in here like friends.

conventional church

And yet, the daffodils, she says.

hates the word - how the speeches start

And yettishness: a state of mind.
rel. is not real

Yettish / myths = (T) saying rel is a myth - not sure as it can b proved

* 2nd voice - normalordinary

O yes, of course the world is harsh,   mocking tone
And suffering, O yes — and yet
This morning, as I walked along
And saw the daffodils, I thought —
And so forth, daffodilling on.

saying evn rel. cant cure / get rid of that
but daffodils make u feel better

her annoyance at pple covering up harsh realities

Easier not to meet each others' eyes.

Rep. = (T) keeps changing her mind,

(T) being critical of this person + believing in daff. as a religion.

And yet, and yes, the daffodils
Making their point, in scuffy gardens,
Beside the lake, beneath the trees,
Municipally distributed, like grit,
Wherever a bulb can lodge and multiply,
Long-legged, gape-mouthed, a yellow hop in air,
Daffodils are.

they're everywhere will - cant cure
harsh reality — similie - like salt on snow
personif.
negative tone - humour - mocking daffodils

            Homelessness, poverty,
Injustice, executions, arms trade, war
Are too.   Says these are real too
            she is angry - daffodils dont help

enjambment - lists

The stillness isn't easy with itself.

daffs. dont solve these—

And yet, and yet.
but they dont try + solve =at least dont pretend 2 solve probs in life

attacking religion, -v real + blunt

*not criticising pple who believe - just the pretense of organised religion

(T) hates falseness
- attacks lack of concern of those who minister religious talks
- contrast religion + reality

*Poem = extended metaphor

61

Atlas

Handwritten annotations (top):
map to book
at athen
or lort

man
mythical greek ~~figure~~ who holds = linked t
the world on his shoulders   physical stren

- huge group of mountains
- deals with love & types of love
not object of love.

represents
ordinary life,
it is importan
although du

Atlas

-to look after
something

There is a kind of love called maintenance,
Which stores the WD40 and knows when to use it;

a noun not person - type of love

Which checks the insurance, and doesn't forget
The milkman; which remembers to plant bulbs;   } thoughtfull

ordinary

Which answers letters; which knows the way
The money goes; which deals with dentists   - important 4
                                              security & health

And Road Fund Tax and meeting trains,
And postcards to the lonely; which upholds

life is ricketty, not smooth

The permanently ricketty elaborate   describes life
Structures of living; which is Atlas.   in a realistic way

talks abt whole world = link to title   their love is safe

And maintenance is the sensible side of love,   true love
Which knows what time and weather are doing   - protects
To my brickwork; insulates my faulty wiring; - keeps safe
Laughs at my dryrotten jokes; remembers
My need for gloss and grouting; which keeps   sets into a house &
My suspect edifice upright in air,   makes it full d
As Atlas did the sky.   protection of
                                              home
fandation to life   root   - physical

all 2 lines each - how
responsible @ is
lover is

constant 2 lines - shows how consistent their love is.

- Atlas is a metaphor for ppl who   * love is real -
  can hold up Fanthorpe's world.   true love isn
  Holding 2gether all the peices.   romantic

- Atlas represents male physical strength - tradicionally

- Attacks chocolate-boxy view of love

- give truthful view d what love shld be.

- Respect for classical/ancient world.

- using ancient wrld to coment on contemporary
                                        society.

62

BOTH A
THINGS.

The Absent-Minded Lover's Apology

[handwritten: not paying attention]
[handwritten: love letter]

I would like you to think I love you *warmly*
Like brown cat yawning among sheets in the linen-cupboard.
[handwritten: similie]
[handwritten: friendly innuendo]
*[handwritten: * rhythm — 1 syllable a word until 2nd voice]*

I would like you to think I love you *resourcefully*
Like rooftop starlings posting chuckles down the flue.

I would like you to think I love you *extravagantly*
Like black cat embracing the floor when you pick up the tin
opener.
[handwritten: sexual innuendo]
[handwritten: idea of warmth sprawled against floor]
[handwritten: hands — shape of (w) legs!]

I would like you to think I love you *accurately*
Like Baskerville kern that fits its place to a T.

I would like you to think I love you *with hurrahs and hallelujahs*
Like dog whippetting at you down the intricate hillside.

I would like you to think I love you *wittily*
Like pottery Cox that lurks in the fruit-bowl under the Granny
Smiths.

I would like you to think I love you *pacifically and for ever*
Like collared doves on the whitebeam's domestic branch.

I would like you to think I love you *chronically*
Like second hand solemnly circumnavigating the clock.

And O I want to love you, not in the absent tense, *but in the here
and the now*
Like a present-minded lover.

*[handwritten: * each stanza except but 2 start same]*
*[handwritten: * last 2 — desire to take over — sounds more urgent.]*

navigation">63

[handwritten: ACTICAL]

AUNT = Aunt - younger than Fanthorpe.
↑ not sister

Themes of innocence vs experience] because jealous?

v. personal

Sister

v. CONTRAST
v. impersonal / detached

First Person

never grows up - childlike - critical of this - not to live in the fantasy world

(She) was a success with dogs, cats, rabbits,
Small, furry, uncritical creatures.

ANIMALS - becoz they lack judgement

Little afterthought, coming behind the do-no-wrong brother, — 1st ch
The brilliant, touchy sister, nothing left for you — 2nd child
3rd child — But the cul-de-sac of immaturity. too much to live up to - trapped in her immaturity

being the youngest

Flirting / childlike - naughty
Always giggling frivolously in corners sly - but childish
With silly friends, or husbands-of-someone-else. - adulthood = no more

more than dismissing!
v. dismissive! - v. horrible
Named after a road, because your mother ⟵ Disparaging
Hadn't really given her mind to it. - an afterthought.
not as interesting as the others

Even the gentle nuns were disappointed: - expect a good child
Your dear sister, always so good at — comparison
1st person ↑ tone changes / Reject empathise btwn siblings / first person / normal!

Elder child of elder daughter, I inherited
You as my younger sister, little aunt - create distance between her & the sist
empathising youngness / being an aunt but ugly grown up.
Who sniggered, and knew nothing, and rebelled
Automatically against the tyranny, the benevolence. - luv or money
ran away to America / u didn't think about what you were doing

America gave you formulae. Returning,
Smudged with accent, *I want out* you'd say,
tantrum! - spoilt - self centred image

Looking around for admiration, like - attention seeker
A clever child, and *No way, no way.*
comparing her to a child

REP. 4 emphasis
No way. You were never going to ripen - we never expected any thing from her
(Dear) little aunt, as a puppy does, or a plum,
v. sarcastic

In spite of the serious husband, godly daughter,
Yours still the horrified eyes of a creature - cant cope with reality
shocked by the world and sheltered by her family

eg: Flowers growing
Trapped in a (magic) unyielding world,
Child of the cul-de-sac.

unexplained

road leads / closed off
DEAD END
v. ambiguous

cant experience life coz she hasn't grown up.

nec to stay young / cant as a adu

idea of being imprisoned

Booz (F) disinherited by dad - rest of fa followed apart from 4 aunt — but aunt is USELESS — Dolls childrens

64

(+ christianity)

directing
it to somebody
very rare

a gift of life →should value life
she was given ↳ live to the full.

→ materialistic presents → irrelevant

Christmas Presents ——

optimism   pun/jolly
→ Christmas, very, have a merry very → cliché of xmas cards
changed   A very merry Christmas, trilled the cards. — ppl say things they
-der   In gynae wards that means: <u>There is a future.</u> dnt mean

gynaecologist - being tested for cancer - still cares about xmas!
of uterus   the meaning

post office
I lay there, while you sorted friends and stamps.
The local wise man had come up with gold: — her true love
The doctor   her gift = her health
A benign cluster. You'll be home by Christmas.   - her life.
it wasn't   she now appreciates
short   cancer! - her xmas present!   life. alliteration
sentence <u>Nothing to say.</u> When I was tired, we held hands. (primary) a spiritual gift
          relieved   remembering when she was   perhaps, she is
          supported by lesbian   in hospital   replacing + with
          partner   something more
But next bed's visitors were staring.   rhet.   solid = her health
<u>Why us?</u> The colour of our hair, perhaps?   q'n.   'life is more
coz of her sexuality   tangable' than
r   isolated/emphasis   (spiritual!
y   You didn't notice, so I didn't tell you. → partner/gift. solid!
happening   she wanted to protect her from the predjudice!
↓
oid   Next day (another day!) her bed was stripped.   died? Solid!
ruth   someone else
       her appreichation for life.   went home??
ays   Her lovers (husband? daughter?) hadn't cared
ind into To watch death creeping up and down her face;   watching someone die -
       Stared at us out of tact, no doubt, — ironic dont know where to look.
omic   Somewhere to rest their <u>smarting eyes</u>, but also
g.   (I like to think) because we were,   they were looking
rackets Of all things, human;   b4 u   at us because it was
social   'sarcastic!   cry   to hard for them
union
       Human, of all things.   Being ironic!!

human life is   very
the most important   harsh!
thing of all!
                                      These ppl / her
                                      dnt think of anger
                                      her as human!

                                      humanity above sexuality
                                      or christianity!

she is saying   * Religion embedded -
that the lesson   xmas relevance
she learnt is   christs birth
that she is
human   trying not to offend
                              they were looking at them
traditional religious   because they didn't want
story of salvation is   to look at the person in the
replaced by real salvation   bed they were visiting!

her being saved in   her salvation is delieved
hospital.   by real people - (water everywhere)

65

Cat in the Manger

In the story, I'm not there.
Ox and ass, arranged at prayer:
But me? Nowhere.

Anti-cat evangelists –
How on earth could you have missed
Such an obvious and able
Occupant of any stable?

Who excluded mouse and rat?
The harmless necessary cat.
Who snuggled in with the holy pair?
Me. And my purr.

Matthew, Mark and Luke and John
(Who got it wrong,
Who left out the cat)
Remember that,
Wherever He went in this great affair,
I was there.

66

Christmas Sounds — *what we have at xmas*

Piano! ①

Boeings wing softly over Earth   *aeroplanes are replacing religious*
Humming like enormous *Messiahs*,   *music*
music played at christmas
Bringing everyone home for Christmas. *Pro Xmas.*

②

Unpleasant
Children (wailing) impossible (wants,   *contradiction that the*
                    planes are bad → presents
Housewives worrying in case enough isn't,   *are good*
Parsons, with prevenient care, sucking Strepsils, *Anti Xmas.*
religious person   *- over worked @ xmas*
onamatapiea   *- negative - hardship.*
Telly jingling twinkling mistletoe-ing,   *meaningless time.*
→ Cash tills recording glad tidings of profit,   *direct quoteation*
Office parties munching through menus —   *of a xmas carol*
                greed.

Crackers! Champagne corks!

At the heart of it all, in the hay,   ①+②+③ = *very loud*
No sound at all but the cattle *The traditional*   *- lots of sounds*
Endlessly chewing it over.   *birth of christ!*   *- chaos*
        pun   *(the celebration*
△ *no sounds.*   *thinking it over.*   *of xmas is*
quiet / peaceful.   *chaotic.*

[left margin vertical: commercialism in general / gritty depiction of the domestic life]

Traditional celebration of xmas — is replaced by
modern concerns of wealth, individualism
       ↓
unlike "xmas presents" it is seen as negative

Seems to respect christ, but not for contempory †.

domestic life in gritty drama.
    ∨
Seems to be everyone doing their own selfish things.

annotation (top): & to an animal which is predjudice against.

annotation: fox hunting - cruel sport?

annotation: giving validity to regional dialect.

annotation: which is predjudice against rual english

The Invitation — *annotation: to christ to join them!*

annotation: all human society = cruel

The Gloucestershire foxes' message
To the child beyond the sea:
We d'hear thee was born in a stable. — *annotation: christ.*
Us dreams uneasy of thee.

annotation: drawing a connection between of the english society & the crowd who crusified christ.

Us knows the pack be after thee,
Us knows how that du end,   *annotation: being part of the crowd has its guilt as well*
The chase, the kill, the cheering,
Dying wi'out a friend.

So lover, us makes this suggestion
To thee and thy fam'ly tu: *annotation: → The invitation.*
Come live wi we under Westridge
Where the huntin folk be few.   *annotation: contrast for the foxes offer and what ppl can offer.*

annotation: Sinister tone! temptation. - the devil!

Thee'll play wi cubs in the sunshine,   *annotation: hope - freedom*
Sleep in our snuggest den,
And feed on — well, us'll see to that —   *annotation: foxes will provide for christ.*
Forget they beastly men.

annotation: awful ← (animal like) irony!

Maybe thee thinks tis too far off,   *annotation: living with foxes it too far off*
Our language strange to thee,   *annotation: different species.*
But remember us foxes of Westridge
When thou tires of humanity.

annotation: 'when' not 'if'

annotation: takes it for granted that christ WILL tire of humanity.

annotation: predjudice of the dispossesed.

annotation: foxes = any dispossesed ppl!

annotation: sympathy for christ = victim of prejudice. ↓ good person.

annotation: ✳ but does Fanthorpe really understand this?

68

The Wicked Fairy at the Manger

My gift for the child:

No wife, kids, home;
No money sense. Unemployable.
Friends, yes. But the wrong sort —
The workshy, women, wogs,
Petty infringers of the law, persons
With notifiable diseases,
Poll tax collectors, tarts;
The bottom rung.
                    His end?
I think we'll make it
Public, prolonged, painful.

Right, said the baby. *That was roughly*
What we had in mind.

History, Tradition + Past

* Haunting - 9
* Silence - 10
* Room - #12
* Tyndale - 14
* Siren Song - 26
* Dying fall - 28
* Reading between - 24
* DNA - 36
* Greensted Church - 40
* Swarkestone - 38

Places

* under the motorway - 42
* Major Rd for Romney - 35
* Grand Union - 37
* Swarkestone - 38
* lost withail in feb - 39
* Greensted Church - 40
* Helpston - 41

Ppl, voices, Attitudes

* Tyndale - 14 -
* Doll's children -
* Counting Song -
* death row poets -
* Unproffessionals -
* DNA
* what in our house.

Poems abt literature / art

* Painter and Poet
* Woman Ironing
* Colophon
* Death Row Poets
* Reading Between
* Tyndale in Darkness
* Lostwithiel in february
* An Easy Day for a lady
* He refuses to read ...

2nd voice
* Painter's poet
* Woman Ironing *
* Odysseus' Cat
* Last House
* He refuses to read ... *

Alert presenter
* painter + poet
* An easy day for a lady

Dispossessed
* Counting song
* Dying fall

ordi things.
* Unproffesionals
* GrandUnion
* Atlas

Humanity/what it is to be hum
* Unproffessionals
* Damage Limitation
* Magic Eyes
* Queening it
* Atlas
* Absent minded ...
* Xmas presents

* He Refuses to read
* Painter and Poet
* Queening it
* Woman Ironing
* Colophon
* Easy Day...
* Sister

Christmas

* Wicked fairy
* Invitation
* Xmas Sounds
* Cat in
* Xmas presents

Religion

* Daffodil Ministry
* Water Everywhere
* Counting Song
* Greensted church
* Deus vs Adam + another
* Damage limitation
* On worms + Being Lucky
* Room where
* Invitation

War

- Siren song
- dying fall   (F) hates war - ruined her childhood life)
- counting song
- Last house
- cotateral Damage.
*

People

* Unproffesional
* An easy day for a lady
* Queening it.
* The Doll's children
* Woman Ironing
* He refuses to read...
* ONA -36
* Counting Song
* Tyndale   14
* What in our house

- para 1 - intro = summy of interp. of ~~poem~~ qu.

- Para 2 - some sort of analysis of poem 1 + 2
  - similarihes in poems - the msg

- Para 3 - talk abt variation of themes
  - (F)'s variation of opinions

- Para 4 - lang, style, structure
  - comparrison/difference
  - comment of (F)'s style
  - AO3

- Para 5 - Your opinion
  - AO4-ur interp of poem

para 6 - Concl
  - explored/shown/told

The Poem →
- voice
- content
- form (eg sonnet, ballad etc)
- tone
- mood
- imagery
- rhythm
- rhyme

A framework for responding to poetry!

AO3 Style
- Onomatopoeia
- sounds — assonance, sibilance
- Alliteration / Assonance
- no rhyme
- half rhyme occasionally
- rhyme
- Personification — Places
- clever writing — hidden meaning, wordplay/pun, extended metaphor
- Titles — PUN-LITERAL, ironic titles (link to msg)
- silent song, Last house
- theme evident here
- final stanzas changes the content of poem

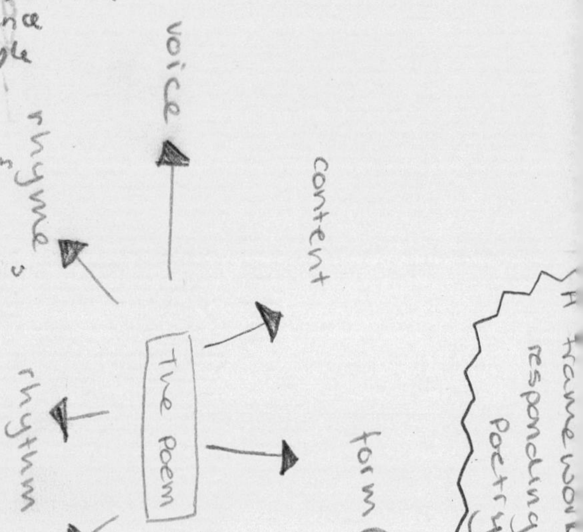

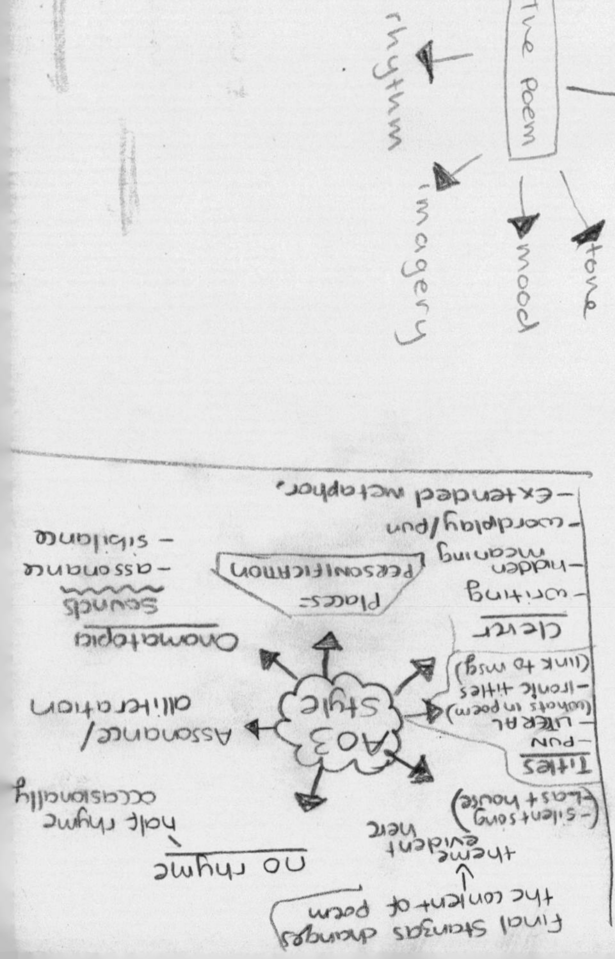